Seven Ways to Look at a Dream

SEVEN WAYS TO LOOK AT A DREAM

by Margot Born

*Illustrated by
Frances Vaughn*

STARRHILL PRESS
Washington & Philadelphia

Published by Starrhill Press, Inc.
P.O. Box 32342
Washington, DC 20007
(202) 686-6703

The author wishes to thank the following: Frances Vaughn, for her delightful illustrations, her helpful comments on the text, and her moral support; Terry Schutz, for providing clarity and organization for her unruly text; Harold Eist and Barbara Hampton, for peopling her dream; and Pat and Dorothy for playing it.

Library of Congress Cataloging-in-Publication Data

Born, Margot.
   Seven ways to look at a dream / Margot Born ; illustrations by
Frances Vaughn. — 1st ed.
     p.   cm.
   Includes bibliographical references (p.   ).
   ISBN 0-913515-73-6: $9.95
   1. Dreams. I. Vaughn, Frances. II. Title.
BF1078.B575 1991
154.6'3—dc20   91-9768
                                       CIP

Printed in the United States of America
First edition

6 5 4 3 2 1

To Alice Large, in memory

And to Edward and Robert Vaughn,
Timothy, Peter, Christopher, Susan and Stephen Born

And to my patients and dream group members,
the real authors of this book

Contents

Tree at my window, window tree,
My sash is lowered when night comes on;
But let there never be curtain drawn
Between you and me.

Vague dream-head lifted out of the ground,
And thing next most diffuse to cloud,
Not all your light tongues talking aloud
Could be profound.

But, tree, I have seen you taken and tossed,
And if you have seen me when I slept,
You have seen me when I was taken and swept
And all but lost.

That day she put our heads together,
Fate had her imagination about her,
Your head so much concerned with outer,
Mine with inner, weather.

– Robert Frost

Introduction

This whole creation [the universe of dreams] is essentially subjective,
and the dream is the theater where the dreamer is at once scene,
actor, prompter, stage manager, author, audience, and critic.
– Carl Gustav Jung, 1928

Whether we remember our dreams or not, we all dream. Dreams are vital to our psychological functioning, and even to our survival. Historically, we have been fascinated, mystified and horrified by dreams. Our dreams, daydreams and fantasies are not bound by the hard realities of waking life. In dreams, images not normally seen together coalesce in ways that some fear are dangerously out of control. Others treasure these combinations of images as evidence of inner riches. For still others, dreams are inspired by supernatural powers. Whatever their source, our dreams are worth getting in touch with because they can help us learn about ourselves and can offer us more choices in life. Dreams broaden our awareness and knowledge of ourselves and of our relationships with others.

Dreams have always served as rich sources of inspiration. There is evidence that prehistoric cave paintings are images from dreams drawn by sorcerers and priests in the belief that their work in some way controlled the prey they drew. In the Old Testament, Joseph's interpretation of Pharaoh's dream initiated the salvation of the Jews from bondage in Egypt. In ancient Greece, Hippocrates used his patients' dreams to help him diagnose and treat their physical ailments. Soothsayers and seers still use dreams to predict the future. Some Senoi tribes in Malaysia achieve peace, harmony and creativity by means of dreams in ways that we will look at later in this book. Robert Louis Stevenson is said to have dreamed the characters and plots of his novels. Einstein reputedly formulated the theory of relativity in a dream.

Dreams have always been interesting to us. Today, in state-of-the-art laboratories, scientists study dreams, dreamers and dream behavior. Yet we still know little more about dreams than the Greeks knew four hundred years before Christ.

What do we know about dreams? We know that our dreams come in cycles. We dream for about a quarter of our sleeping time every night, and our dreams are interspersed with ninety- or hundred-minute cycles of nondreaming sleep. Our dreaming periods are marked by rapid eye movements (REMs). We know that when we are deprived of dreams, we wake up after eight or ten hours of sleep feeling unrested. If dream deprivation is prolonged, we may become irritable, irrational, even psychotic. This is evidence that dreaming is essential to our physical and psychological well-being.

It seems that dreams function as internalizers and organizers of sensory stimuli that we experience during the day. These events need to be integrated into the structure of our experience, so that we can make sense of ourselves in our world. In other words, dreams help us make internal sense of the many random experiences that we have had during the day. These

experiences can then enter our lifelong flow of experience, both internal and external, without overwhelming us with their quantity and the chaos of their randomness. We then can integrate them into the accumulation of experience that constitutes our sense of ourselves in the world.

The process of looking at our dreams seems to strengthen us and to make our sense of self firmer and more trustworthy. We need only take a little time to look at and explore our dreams to come to appreciate them, to uncover some of our own inner workings and to discover parts of ourselves that are most valuable and, above all, most completely our own. We can then become more competent and efficient agents of our action, feeling and thinking. As we gain more trust in ourselves, we depend less on the temporary, external and often futile expedients that we tend to use to shore up our conflicts, ignorance, neediness and other inevitable discomforts and dissatisfactions of life. We seek satisfaction less in material things beyond what we need and can concentrate more on our inner needs, conflicts and resources.

This book is about discovering what your dreams mean to you. You are the ultimate expert in examining your dreams. No one—not me, Sigmund Freud or Carl Jung—can tell you more about your dreams than you can tell yourself. If you let yourself see, feel, smell and hear and allow memories and meanings to arise from your own inner sources of creativity, you will achieve great results.

I will describe and illustrate, with a dream of my own, seven ways of looking at dreams. Other people have found these methods helpful, interesting, therapeutic, laughable, terrifying, or almost anything else you can imagine. Some of them are of ancient origin; some are enlargements and extensions of Freud's turn-of-the-century discovery of dreams as the "royal road to the unconscious." Some will be useful or amusing or important to you, and some may offer you little or nothing.

This is a simple manual, a gentle companion to dreaming, that can suggest new ways of learning about yourself. It is not meant to be a rule book or to tell you the "right" and "wrong" of dreaming or working with dreams. Because dreams are evocative and speak to us on many levels, this book is a tool for evoking some of our own mysteries, not a provider of answers. It is meant to be, like dreams themselves, imaginative and playful. If it can help you to regard yourself with humility, a fresh mind and childlike curiosity, it will have accomplished a large part of its task.

Whether you use this book for help in everyday, practical problem solving, as a guide on a spiritual quest, or, as a friend who lives alone put it, "company in bed," I hope you find it helpful, enlightening, enriching, or just plain fun. May it bring you many friends and many adventures! What follows are two brief sections intended to equip you for a journey into your dreams and then, one by one, seven methods of understanding dreams.

Remembering and Recording Your Dreams

It is not wisdom to be only wise
And on the inward vision close the eyes.

— George Santayana

You may be one of the many people who believe they don't dream. You do dream, and you can easily learn techniques to help you remember your dreams.

Most people begin to remember dreams when they read a book about dreaming. Simple interest seems to spark the ability to remember. And when they dream, they tend to dream in images that correspond to the theory they are reading about. After reading Freud, their dreams tend to contain Freudian material; after reading Jung, Jungian.

To remember your dreams, it is helpful first to tell yourself at night that you will remember your dream. Then you may need to set aside a quiet time between waking up and getting up to think about what you dreamed. Often just a few minutes of reflection and relaxation will allow memories to surface. If you draw a blank, lie in the position in which you woke up or, even better, the one in which you dreamed. Fantasizing that you are still asleep may jog your memory.

Any fragmentary image is useful. If one comes, explore it. You will often find that the dream arises spontaneously when you begin to associate freely to even a tiny glimpse of it. Since a dream is your own production, nourished by a source within you, you may garnish, embellish or fantasize with the same abandon that the dream had. Complete accuracy in remembering is not important. Sometimes failure of memory can evoke fanciful fillings in of blank spaces, which are nourished by the same inner source as the dream.

The alarm clock, physical or emotional pressures, or the demands of the waking day may erase conscious memory of the dream despite a willing spirit. You can help yourself remember your dreams by setting your alarm clock a little earlier for a few days, then setting it back to the regular time. You will probably continue to wake up at the earlier time. The interval between waking up and the ringing of the alarm is "free" time in which you may be able to remember your dream.

If you set aside a block of time upon waking up to give your dreams a chance to emerge, eventually you will remember them. If you can't change your schedule to accommodate dream reminiscence, you can substitute a waking fantasy or daydream for a dream and study it according to the methods presented here.

16

If prolonged effort to recall your dreams remains unsuccessful, rather than intrusively push through your forgetfulness, you may want to examine what is going on. Forgetting may have an important meaning in itself. Respect it when it occurs. It may be protecting you from overwhelming or difficult knowledge that is still too painful to deal with. For example, people who have been sexually or violently abused often cope with what might be unbearable by forgetting or denying the abuse. This enables them to take from the abuser, who may be a parent, the emotional nourishment that they need to survive. A dream might evoke the memory of the abuse before the person is able to handle it or while he or she still feels the need for emotional nourishment from someone who would, if the truth were known, seem too dangerous to trust. Forgetting, in this kind of situation, can be a lifesaving defense, one that blots out the possibility that someone depended on is not trustworthy. Almost everyone blots out memories that are emotionally threatening. Forgetting in such instances is protective.

Occasionally, uncovered dream material causes such stress or anxiety that it is hard to handle alone. If this happens to you, do not pressure yourself. You may want to find someone with psychological training who is experienced in handling dream material to help guide you through it.

Usually, however, a quiet, floating awareness of your morning awakenings will clear your consciousness of some of the interferences and provide a clean surface that is receptive to dream memories. You will remember a dream eventually. When you do, be alertly ready for it. It might be a good idea to keep a notebook and pencil or a tape recorder by your bed.

When a dream is remembered, be ready for what it offers with as few preconceptions as possible. Rigid preconceptions don't allow space for new perceptions to enter our consciousness.

17

Other techniques for remembering dreams are more intrusive than those I usually recommend to my patients and my dream groups. I am cautious about them, but for those who are more action oriented than I am, these methods can be rewarding.

Here, then, are a few technical suggestions for remembering your dreams. You will need to find out for yourself whether the more passive or more active approach suits you better. Begin by letting the dream speak for itself as much as possible. If it refuses, then you can go on to using alarms and tape recorders. Here are some techniques:

1. As you go to sleep, repeat, either aloud or silently, "Tonight I will remember a dream. Tonight I will remember a

dream," until you feel relaxed enough to induce a sort of self-hypnotic trance and go to sleep. Even if you don't remember the dream, the relaxation will be good for you.

2. Sleep less during the night and take naps at other times. Often shorter sleeps produce more memories of dreams, but the dreams seem to be different in quality from late-night dreams. There is evidence to suggest that early-night dreams and nap dreams deal more with the residue of the current day. Later-night dreams deal more with deeper, earlier levels of your life. So if you work on remembering dreams from naps, don't worry if the dreams seem trivial or factual repetitions of the day's events. You are only learning how to remember at this point. Besides, it is interesting to ask what it is about a particular event in your day, whether trivial or momentous, that caused your dream to pick it up.

3. Set an alarm clock for every two or three hours during the night. Immediately write down or tape-record the dream you catch.

4. If you still have no dream memories, use fantasies, daydreams, or any other part of your creative imagination, or use your inner vision. These mental creations can be examined in the same ways as dreams.

We don't know where our dreams come from, but we do have some influence on where they go. We remember and use our dreams well when we are open to our hearts, heads, noses, ears, mouths and less exalted sense organs, which might speak to us when we are quiet enough to listen. Our dreams often give answers to our questions about our lives. So let us not just gaze, but feel, smell, taste and hear as we provide the conditions in which new experiences can be bred: a quiet attentiveness, an inward gaze and a listening stance. Then, as William Faulkner writes in *Absalom, Absalom,* you, "the dreamer, clinging yet to the dream, sharpen the savor, waking into the reality, the more than reality, not the unchanged and unaltered old time, but into a time altered to fit the dream."

When you return, however reluctantly, from your dream journey to the harsh light of waking reality, you will bring with you a new dimension as you put your two feet firmly on the cold, hard floor, brush your teeth and manage your life.

When you have stayed with your dream awhile, observing and sharpening your awareness, you will feel ready to go on. As Rainer Maria Rilke writes, "The work of sight is done. Now do heart work on the pictures that are within you."

Recording Your Dream

Now that you have produced a dream, a daydream or a fantasy to work with, you may wonder how to catch and hold it. Here, again, make your own decision with deference to your unconscious. However, don't delay or you will lose the dream. Until you have either mentally or physically registered the dream, don't get up, don't talk to anyone, and don't do anything except lie in bed for a few minutes alone with your dream.

Some say that to write a dream down is already to lose its true essence, which is ephemeral. Others find writing such an arduous duty that the mere prospect may interfere with the remembering. It is true that translating something visual into words and then into writing distorts and eliminates some of the qualities of the original. If you don't want to write your dream down, scrutinize it, at first without giving it meanings. Just follow along with the plot line, as though you were watching an interesting film or reading a story. Later on you will be able to see and know the dream from many new viewpoints and on many levels.

If you decide that you want to write down your dreams,

keep a notebook and pen beside your bed. An attractive notebook seems to attract interesting dreams. It is a beautiful container waiting to be filled.

For some people, just turning on the light to find pen and pad may erase the dream memory. In this case, a small bedside tape recorder with glow-in-the-dark tape on its "record" button may be the answer. For those who don't want to disturb bedmate or roommate, a pencil with a built-in flashlight can be bought.

The intransigent balker at recording a dream, either on paper or tape, probably has some valid conscious or unconscious reasons for balking. If recording a dream is too great a struggle, you are probably telling yourself that your dreams are better left unrecorded for the time being. Remember that it is the process of working on dreams and an awareness of yourself as a dreamer rather than a final complete dream interpretation that you want to develop in the beginning. It maybe enough for you to remember and begin to record a few images from your dream.

As you record the dream, or repeat it to yourself, try to reexperience the dreaming as closely as possible. Thinking of it or recording it in the present tense ("I go to a dance. I meet an attractive person") helps here.

In my opinion, no dream is too trivial, too wicked, too bizarre or too mundane to merit the dreamer's attention. These "toos" are value judgments from the rationally discriminatory waking brain; they do not apply to the irrational, nondiscriminatory dream life. If, at first glance, your dream seems unworthy of attention, it will often reap rich rewards if you can suspend judgment long enough to listen to it with an open mind and naive consciousness. Important latent, or hidden, themes are often disguised by the manifest, or apparent, content of the dream. Because dreams are fantasies and not actions, they can do no harm and therefore have no moral value. A dream that may initially appear trivial or wicked to you can become an exciting and important adventure or a powerful force toward self-understanding.

A dream can be recorded in many ways, depending on what you want to do with it later. Here are a few general guidelines that you may want to put in your dream journal as headings, or keep at your bedside to refer to as you write or talk into your machine. These are the basics. You may want to spend a few weeks recording dreams in this way before going on to try some of the techniques that stress exploration of different dream elements. You probably will need to set aside at least fifteen minutes every morning for this task.

1. Record the dream in the present tense, which intensifies and gives immediacy to the experience you had.
2. Note the setting with care. Drawing or diagraming may be easier than writing out. Are there any bizarre elements or incongruities? If so, note them. They often turn out to be the most revealing or most amusing parts of the dream.
3. Who are the characters in the dream and what do they do? Are you one of the actors? An observer? You can ask the same questions about the nonhuman elements of the dream, which often turn out to symbolize human characteristics, or people you know.
4. What is the mood of the dream? Note it briefly. Does the mood change as the dream unfolds?
5. Is the dream in color? Are you aware of any nonvisual sensations such as texture or temperature, comfort or pain?

When you have a group of dreams recorded or thought about in this way, you will be ready to go on to the next chapter on the use of dreams to help solve problems. In that chapter I relate a dream that I will use as an illustration in the rest of the book. It is my own dream, as it must be, because I can interpret with authority only my own dreams, and even that is sometimes questionable. You will find it helpful to become familiar with my dream so that you won't have to keep referring back to it each time I look at it from a new perspective.

Each of the following chapters presents a particular viewpoint of dreams. The views are different, but they share many characteristics, too. Each chapter begins by listing what the approach it presents offers the dreamer. Leaf through! Choose any method you want! Any chapter that serves your purpose will do. You may find that different approaches suit different dreams. Or you may like some approaches very much and not like others at all. You may end up with an amalgam of ideas from all or most of the methods presented here complemented by a large infusion of your own intuition.

This book can serve as a sort of seed catalog of methods of dream analysis; browse through it, remembering that all the methods require some nurturing, watering and fertilizing.

If you prefer, think of the book as a travel brochure or guide to dream lands. The descriptions may be appealing, but you still have to go to the places yourself to believe and experience what the book talks about.

And now that you are equipped for the journey, let's embark. All aboard!

CHAPTER I

Problem Solving:
A Practical Approach to Dreams

Training your dreams to produce practical, commonsense solutions to day-to-day or long-term problems is the goal of the practical way of looking at dreams. With a little knowledge and only a few weeks of practice, you can learn how to simplify and clarify the issues of a problem, incubate a dream and work on that dream to lead yourself to the answer you need.

These techniques are part of the most ancient of dream traditions, and the most modern. In ancient Greece, oracles taught dream incubation techniques. Today, techniques like these based on research on the functions of the left and right hemispheres and other parts of the brain are at the cutting edge of dream science.

These methods are based on two assumptions. The first is that we can control the content of our dreams to the extent that we can influence them to deal with subjects we want them to address. Oracles in ancient Greece made this same assumption. The practice it produces is called "dream incubation." In Greece, pilgrims went to oracles, who taught them how to incubate dreams to get help of many sorts. Dreams were used to diagnose and learn how to cure a wide variety of physical and emotional illnesses, to predict or influence future events, to help make decisions, to promote fertility and for many other purposes.

The second assumption is that the reputedly more intuitive, creative and irrational right hemisphere of our brain and the practical, rational and linguistic left hemisphere have valuable advice to offer each other. Although much is yet to be learned about the physiology of the brain, the concept that the two hemispheres function differently is useful to us as we study our own dreams and work to integrate the parts of ourselves that are split off from or ignorant of each other. Whether we ask ourselves for solutions to general or specific problems, whether we seek figurative, symbolic answers or literal, concrete answers, if we persevere in the practice of these techniques, we will find them useful and productive.

To begin this process, we incubate a dream. We plant a dream seed. This means that we conceive and nurture an idea, an issue, or a problem until a dream dealing with our chosen subject hatches.

Begin by finding a quiet place in which you allow the issues that are concerning you to float into your consciousness and delineate themselves. Ancient dreamers found a sacred place, often a quiet grove, a place where nothing everyday happened and where there were no interruptions. They lay and slept or meditated until the god of the particular temple precincts in which they were incubating their dream visited them in a dream or a vision and gave their task definition. Whether you wait for a force outside you or your own inner voice to speak, the process will be passive unless you already have a burning issue begging for resolution.

Relax in a comfortable chair or lie down. The passivity that you acquire by relaxing helps you become receptive and open so that you can hear and see your often unrecognized introspective self. This practice in receptivity and openness will serve you well later, too, when you need to adopt the same sort of free-floating, open awareness toward the dream you will produce. Give yourself plenty of time.

The choice of areas that you can explore is virtually limitless. Your issue can be interpersonal, creative or spiritual. It can involve yourself, your family or your work. You may want to shed more light on a possible career change, choose a marriage partner or find a creative solution to an artistic or professional problem. You may just want to make a better pancake. Any or all of these areas may be investigated and their meanings to you widened and deepened through incubation and exploration of a dream.

Choose only one issue at a time, and try to stick with it until you strike pay dirt. You may need to reframe your question or adjust it, but stay with the basic issue you started with if possible. If not possible, follow the digression with interest.

When you have framed and articulated the area in which you want to learn something, frame your question about it as clearly and succinctly as you can.

Once you have a short phrase or question specifying clearly what you want from your dream, relax deeply from the tips of your toes to the crown of your head and repeat your request over and over again. After coming out of your relaxation period, repeat the request from time to time as you go about your daily routine. When you go to bed, put a pencil and paper (or whatever recording device you have chosen) by your bed in readiness and repeat the phrase you have decided upon until you go to sleep. In the morning, if you are aware of having had a dream—any dream, whether it seems immediately relevant or not—record it, either in writing or on tape. For those who have trouble remembering in the morning, it is a good idea to wake up and record the dream immediately after dreaming, regardless of the time of night (or day) the dream occurs and despite any irrelevance, stupidity or triteness it may seem to have. If you have asked for help with a relationship, and you get a dream about split pea soup, do not reject the dream. The split pea soup may relate, on closer examination, both to your request for help (the soup is comforting) and to the ominous possibility that your relationship is over (the peas are split).

To demonstrate what I have been telling you, I incubated the dream I describe below and discovered much that was helpful to me when I explored what the dream was telling me. You may follow along with the same process for a dream of your own.

To incubate the dream, I lay in the sun in the garden, watching the clouds float by. I achieved almost complete relaxation as thoughts about this book floated into consciousness, just as the clouds floated in and out of view above me. Gradually my thoughts focused on something I wanted for this book, an idea about a way to show readers clearly how they might use their own dreams. After framing several wordy or unclear questions to ask my dreaming self, I settled on this request: "Please give me a dream that will illustrate the process of exploring and understanding dreams clearly to my readers." I repeated this request to myself several times over the course of the next two or three days and went to bed each evening with a clear mind. In bed, I repeated my request again and again until I went to sleep. Nothing happened. In fact, I stopped remembering any dreams at all for about a week. I realized that I needed either to rework the problem, to rephrase my request or to forget the book.

After further relaxation and free association, I wondered what it was that stopped me from remembering a helpful sample dream, or any dream at all for that matter. The new phrase I repeated over and over again was, "Please tell me what is stopping me from remembering my dreams. Does it mean I shouldn't try to write the book?" Again, I woke up with nothing and felt discouraged and frustrated.

However, as I was washing my breakfast dishes one morning, enjoying the bubbles of detergent and the warm water, a knife handle emerging through the suds gave rise to the image of interesting though unidentifiable objects emerging from a deep, tightly packed tote bag. Alerted by the vividness and detail of the image, I realized that I was remembering a recent dream. I thought about the dream in the present tense. It didn't, at first glance, seem to have anything to do with my question, but I knew that dreams often disguise their true subject. When my memory of the dream began to flow smoothly, I sat down to record it. This is what I wrote:

> I am at a conference in the country, maybe in the Berkshires. It's autumn, and most of the leaves have fallen. Three of us are sitting together in a large conference room talking about how many full days of the conference are left and when we will come back for another. Other clusters of people are here and there in this large hall, murmuring in the background. The three people in my group are a woman I don't know; my friend, Barbara, a friend and colleague from my clinic, and myself. Beside Barbara's chair, on the floor, is her tote bag. It is neatly and snugly packed with objects that I feel are extremely interesting, although I can't really see what they are. I can only see the tops of them. However, no matter how much I want to, it is out of the question for me to ask Barbara what she has in her purse. A woman, another stranger, strides over to us, reaches down into Barbara's bag and, with complete confidence, grasps two little pouches. She snatches them out. I am somewhat aghast that she has brazenly intruded in this way, but Barbara doesn't seem to mind. The woman opens the two little pouches in front of the whole assemblage and not only reveals, but holds up for all to see, a mass of disks, cones, chess pawns and other objects connected by ganglia-like rubbery threads and veins. The grabber says, in a very businesslike way, "These are calipers to measure the brain. One set is for children, and the other is for adults." The woman beside me is horrified and gasps, "People aren't allowed to know about these things." I ask, "Why not?" and she says, "It's terribly esoteric," in an awed voice. Barbara laughs and says, "Oh, it's all right. Although you have to be cautious with the grown-ups' calipers. The children's are okay. Even Harold says so."

27

After I wrote down the dream, I named the two strangers. The woman who swept down upon us is called Brazen Hussy. The priggish woman is the nosy Goody Two-Shoes.

At this point, you will probably notice that this business of incubating a dream to solve a problem may become a problem in itself. Having incubated a dream to help me write a book, I was by no means finished. I still had to wait for clarity about how to use the dream to illustrate the ways of working with dreams. The work of listening to what the dream was saying was really just beginning. However, what I had done up to this point had been in itself worthwhile. I was able to remember a dream and write it down.

The next task before me, interestingly, was not to know too much. When I knew too much, I almost dismissed the dream as irrelevant. Superficially, it made no reference to dreams, dreaming or the problem I had incubated it for. Nothing seemed to connect it to the issues I was dealing with.

If you bear with me, you will see how my dream emerged for me. If you are working on a dream of your own, your dream may emerge in a similar way. If you have been following this process with a dream incubation and recording, you are now ready to begin to work with your own dream material.

To approach my dream as openmindedly as possible, I put aside my request for a dream and pretended to myself that I had not incubated this dream. I was ready to begin a more or less methodical investigation into why I had this dream now and what it had to say to me.

The first step was to ask myself questions about the dream. These questions, and their answers, need to emanate from the most naive, innocent and ignorant state achievable. I began with some questions about the setting, which was the Berkshires in late autumn, when the leaves have nearly all fallen. Even though the action takes place indoors, I am aware of and can even see the landscape surrounding our conference

room. I asked many more questions than I include here. This is a sample.

Q: *What are mountains?*
A: Mountains are what happens when the earth rises up into the sky to a peak. They can be enormous. In the mountains, the air is crisp and clear. It is quiet there and voices echo. There are dark pine trees that smell pungent. In winter, there is snow. In summer, the air is cool. In autumn, the leaves are spectacularly colored. Everything looks sharp and clear there. [Although the qualities described here are more or less general, another person, asked the same question, might describe different qualities based on different experiences of mountains.]

Q: *What are these mountains?* [Asking how some element in the dream is different from all other members of the class of objects or persons it belongs to often elicits important information.]
A: They are the Berkshires, in western Massachusetts. These mountains are spectacularly red, orange and black in autumn. I spent my high school years in boarding school there. What is peculiar to the Berkshires for me is how I felt when I lived there. I felt secure and safe enough to be creative with abandon. Those years were happy ones for me, at least at school. I was experimenting with lots of ways of being, and with doing lots of new creative things, painting, writing, acting, working with various materials to make things and learning with great gusto.

29

I now had set up the broad context and the mood of the dream. I was satisfied with the results of my work so far. The dream began to seem auspicious, but it is important to be cautious in judging this quality. Dreams that seem promising can lead to dead ends. Apparent inauspiciousness or auspiciousness deserves skepticism and should not influence the decision to discontinue or continue work on a dream.

I moved on to the smaller, microcosmic context of my dream, the conference room.

Q: *What is a conference room?* [Again, notice the naiveté of the questioner. The question is about the general class or characteristics of an element of the dream.]

A: A conference room is a room where people meet to hear lectures, to confer, to have workshops. It is a meeting place.

Q: *What is this particular conference room?*

A: In this case, although I call it a conference room, the room is large enough to be an assembly or lecture hall. It is a large amphitheater with seats arranged in semicircular tiers descending to a speaker's platform. I don't remember ever having been in this hall before, but it's like one I knew as an undergraduate at Harvard. Or another one at a conference of the Association for the Study of Dreams that I went to last summer. But the people in it are not from those places. Barbara and I are sitting in the front row, near the empty speaker's rostrum. I believe the speaker has spoken and left. But quite a few people are still clustered about in the auditorium. They seem to be waiting for something.

Q: *What is the mood of the conference room?*

A: The mood of this smaller, interior setting, unlike the mountains outside, is somewhat threatening. I feel as though I ought to be on my best public behavior. I also feel vulnerable to criticism and, at the same time, voraciously curious about what's in Barbara's bag, which is right next to me, almost against my leg. I can only see the tops of objects, which are packed in the bag lengthwise. But because I feel threatened, I can't ask about them or touch them.

Q: *Who is Barbara?*

A: [I am going to describe Barbara first as I know her in waking life.] Barbara is a friend and colleague, a psychologist who works at the same clinic as I do, someone who won't put up with nonsense. She is also a writer. I liked her last staff presentation, which was about dreams, and I especially like her sense of humor. She has a collection of quotations that she offered to let me look at and use for my dream book. We went to a course together on the use of dreams in psychoanalysis. I had talked to her briefly at our clinic symposium on the day before I had the dream.

Q: *Who is Barbara in the dream?*
A: She looks cool and contained. She punctures the self-important priggishness of Goody Two-Shoes, whose voice has a sort of "naughty-naughty" tone, by laughing at her comment. She doesn't even take Harold, the highly respected head of our clinic, too seriously. When she says, in my dream, "Even Harold says so," there is a faintly ridiculing tone in her voice. She seems to imply that the strictness of Harold's standards, which he sometimes presents in an overbearing way, makes it hard to get his okay. However, he has approved the showing of the contents of at least one pouch, an approval made unnecessary by the tone and implication of Barbara's comment. Barbara also makes fun of those of us who take authority too seriously. Her serenity and humor provide a holding structure for her last comment, which subtly embodies ambivalence toward authority—the conflict between fear of authority and longing for it—and the suggestion that authority must be taken into one's own hands. [The theme that Barbara has introduced here offers infinite possibilities for a lifetime of expansion, but I have incubated this dream to solve a particular problem. The Barbara of the dream helps me write my book by giving me permission to take authority into my own hands.]

Q: *Who is Brazen Hussy, who goes directly to Barbara's bag and takes out the two pouches?*
A: I don't know her. She has no fear whatsoever and dares do anything she likes without regard for manners or the opinion of others. She knows how to get what she wants. She just takes it and doesn't care whether it belongs to someone else.

Q: *And what is a pouch?*
A: A pouch holds things snugly, and the things in it are apt to be precious. It is soft and flexible and has a drawstring, and it fits into places easily. It holds a lot for its size and,

when empty, can fold up into hardly any space at all. It is a useful, easy-to-make container. If you lost your purse, you could easily make a pouch out of a piece of cloth. It's a sort of detached pocket.

Q: *What are the two pouches in the dream?*
A: They are made of a rubbery substance, something like a membrane. Empty, they remind me of placentas; full, of brains. Also, like placentas, they seem to hold something about to be born, and, like brains, they seem to hold the capacity to think and dream.

Q: *And the networks of ganglia that hold the objects together? What are ganglia? [What is important here is not the scientific meaning of "ganglia," but the dreamer's definition of the term.]*
A: Ganglia are connecting filaments. They are fine, even hairlike. I think of them as part of our nervous system, especially in the brain, but I think they also connect all the parts of the nervous system in the whole body.

Q: *And the shapes, the disks, the pawns and the other objects that the ganglia connect?*
A: They are different from each other but connected, something like blood platelets or different types of brain cells or functions. They are things that do various tasks, I think, or serve various purposes. But they have quite clear, nonorganic-looking geometric shapes in this dream.

Q: *What are calipers?*
A: They are devices to measure the thickness of three-dimensional objects.

Q: *And these calipers?*
A: As displayed by Brazen Hussy, the contents of the pouches resemble objects measurable by calipers, and she says they are calipers to measure the brain. To me, they seem like models of the brain itself. I think what Brazen Hussy means is that exposure of the brain reveals a great deal—as much as measuring it with calipers would reveal. Like calipers, exposure reveals the brain's size or capacity in

32

three dimensions.

In the dream, one of the calipers is for measuring children's brains and one is for measuring adults' brains.

Q: *What are children's brains?*
A: A child's brain is young and innocent. [As the dream unfolds it becomes clear that the meaning of brain and mind overlap. You will find many such blurrings of meaning in your dreams and they will often be useful, though sometimes confusing.] Because the child is not yet aware of what it is to be responsible, he can't yet be blamed for his motivations or actions. He is still allowed to make mistakes, still in the learning stage. His brain has an enormous capacity to absorb knowledge. He can show wider and more untrammeled ranges of emotion than adults can. His brain has tremendous potential.

Q: *And what is the child's brain in the dream?*
A: Because of this child's innocence, it's okay for his brain—his thinking and his emotional parts—to be exposed to the world. He's allowed to make mistakes, and no one is bothered much by them, or by their exposure. He's still in the learning stage of life. Anyone can see all of the dream brain's connections and inner workings when the woman takes it out of the pouch. The child can be transparent without being rejected or punished in some way for what has been divulged about him.

Q: *And what are adults' brains?*
A: An adult's brain is different from a child's. It has things to hide. An adult has to be responsible and to think clearly in a logical, sensible way. If an adult's brain or mind doesn't work this way—and, of course, it doesn't—exposure can be embarrassing, even painful. However, the fear of exposure and not what is exposed is the problem. An adult has built up an image of a reputation that, even if it is pure fantasy, needs to be protected.

Q: *And the brain of the adult in the dream?*
A: Exposed for all the world to see.

Q: *How does this dream seem connected with anything happening in your life now?*

A: The Berkshires remind me of when I was there, doing a lot of reading, writing and painting, learning how to do things, experimenting with energy and excitement, all with little fear of the judgment of others. I was too excited about the processes themselves, the high feeling of experimentation, of getting to know new writers, the qualities of paint, and the energy of adolescent sexuality. I was exploring the world with a child's eyes and brain and curiosity and was on an exhilarating learning kick, taking my first steps in new worlds. Now I am writing a book and have not done any writing for years. I feel unskilled, like a toddler or that adolescent, but with adult fears like those of Goody Two-Shoes.

The particular wide-open out-of-doors with its heady mountain air evokes the exhilaration of creativity of my adolescence. As I work on this part of my dream, I can feel the old creative energy begin to flow. The energy flows, but the words don't, inhibited by adult fears of irresponsibility, exposure of sexuality, and taking authority into my own hands.

The conference room takes on the role of organizer and censor in this free mountain setting. In it, the energy will not be out of control. Here I have to be adult and responsible. The dream has exposed my conflicts between creativity and responsibility, sexual energy and repression, and many others. No longer untrammeled as in my childhood, these conflicts have to be reckoned with if I am to go on with the book.

I also have to write a book that will be open to the world's scrutiny, and I have chosen to discuss in it a dream from my most interior and private life, my dream world. The people who will scrutinize me are the people from my clinic, professional colleagues (Barbara), the Association for the Study of Dreams (the conference room is the one where the association met), and the world in general (Brazen Hussy, who knows nothing about anything and has no inhibitions). The capacity of my brain will be measured (calipers) by all these people. Not only my adult brain, but the childish, foolish parts of me will be exposed (child's brain).

Worse still, as I work on the dream the links between creativity and sexuality emerge more and more powerfully, and I blush. It becomes clear that on some level I experience any sort of creative act as if it were related to the primal sexual act. Even though I know it isn't objectively true, writing seems at times to be an act of flagrant sexual exhibitionism, and it arouses the shame of being caught in the act. It isn't clear whether the shamefulness of the offense derives from sexuality itself or from the exhibiting of it.

Barbara, who owns the tote bag, is there to help me not take myself too seriously and to offer useful and interesting information (contained in her tote bag full of interesting objects). Even if my worst fears of too much self-exposure (the horror of Goody Two-Shoes) are confirmed, if I'm laughed at, rejected or exposed as incompetent, it won't make much difference (as the Brazen Hussy, who can do anything, shows me). So I might just as well go ahead and give birth (the sacs containing the ganglia and the different shapes resemble wombs).

The different ways we can look at dreams (different shapes) now appear to be connected by my own knowledge and emotion as well as by the dream I have dreamed. They are connected by many threads (the ganglia), and they will now not get out of control because they are restrained by the ganglia and also contained by the pouches and the tote bag.

Without pursuing this dream much further in detail here (I'm going to subject the same dream to other approaches in subsequent chapters), you can see that it relates very much to my project of writing a book about dreams.

One final mark of understanding a dream, a test you can subject your dream work to, is to see that every element in the dream fits. If there is anything left hanging, that won't harmonize, then meanings may have prematurely been forced onto it. Go back to the beginning of the dream work, and become as ignorant as possible again.

The last question to apply to this and all dreams you work with in this method is:

Q: *How can I apply what I have learned from the dream to my waking life and the problem I incubated the dream to address?*

A: I am going to make this dream the connecting membrane of the chapters of my book. As we compare, contrast and learn about different ways of looking at a dream, we can expect different results from different treatments of dreams. This dream will be a sample. My readers' own dreams will be the chief objects of their explorations, which will be led by different tour guides, Carl Jung, the Senoi, Fritz Perls and others. The reader will learn and invent ways to guide a tour of his own dreams.

In brief, and step by step, this is the method I have used in this problem-solving or practical approach to dreams:

1. Establish the setting of the dream and its general atmosphere.

2. Ask yourself questions about the general qualities of each character or object as though you had never seen such a character or object before. For example, "What is dog?" About people whom you know in reality, ask what in a very general way they mean or suggest to you in real life. About Barbara, I might ask, "What is a psychologist?"

3. Then ask specifically about the character or object in your dream, what makes this object different from all others in its class? For example, "What is this dog?" and "What is this dog to you?"

4. Ask yourself what role each character or object plays in your dream.

5. When you have dealt with all the parts of the dream and the roles the people and objects play in it, ask how the dream relates to the question you used to incubate it.

6. Finally, how can you apply the dream to your life and specifically to the problem you have incubated the dream to address?

Writing on the following work sheet or following it as a guide may also be helpful to you.

Worksheet
Problem Solving

Incubate a dream by taking some quiet time to ask:
What area of life do I feel I'd like help in?

What concise question do I want my dream to try to answer?

As you fall asleep, ask yourself for a dream that addresses these questions. When the dream comes, write it down.

Your dream:

Now, think about each part of the dream:
How do you experience being in the dream setting?

What is this setting to you?

What general, or class of, qualities does each person or
thing in the dream have?

What is particular about each person or thing in your dream?

How do you feel about each person, place or thing?

What is the plot line of the dream, the action?

How is this action related to something that's going on in your life now?

What part of your waking life feelings do your feelings in your dream resemble?

When all the pieces of the dream puzzle fit together, ask:
How does the dream relate to the dream incubation question, or to the area of my life that I want to dream about?

What have you learned from this dream that you can use in solving the problem of your dream incubation question?

CHAPTER II

The Senoi Approach to Dreams:
A Way to Harmony

Know transformation through and through.
What experience has been most painful to you?
If the drinking's bitter, turn to wine.

— Rainer Maria Rilke

To work toward integrating your inner fantasy world and your dream life with your waking activities; to find courage in the face of frightening situations; to learn new ways to look at yourself, your world and its inhabitants and to bring these elements into harmony; to find the sweet wine in the bitter and the bitter in the sweet, the order in apparent chaos or the chaos in order, the victory in defeat or the defeat in victory; to uncover unacknowledged, forbidden wishes so that they can work for you instead of against you; to bring some of the pleasures of the night into the day, where they can be applied creatively; to enhance the value of your dreams and, thereby, your feeling of self-worth: these are some of the objectives of the Senoi method of interpreting dreams.

The Senoi, a people now mythologized by dream scholars of the West, live deep in the remote jungles of Malaysia. This tribe seeks to unify what most of us look at as separate realms of existence—fantasy life, family life and the larger societal life—through dreams. They are a peaceful, harmonious and creative people. It is believed that they achieve these qualities by seeking out and dealing with their antitheses in dreams. The Senoi are encouraged to experience enmity, hostility, fear and any other uncomfortable or disruptive emotions fully in their dreams and, by exploring their dreams, to find peace, friendship, love and courage. A creative work or action or an idea that can be applied to daily life is the end product of dream exploration. Sometimes, with the help of family and tribal council, a person can use a dream to make important decisions or contributions to the tribe or even the nation.

The Senoi also use their dreams to resolve intrapsychic conflict and to regulate interpersonal relationships and tribal affairs. Their methods of dream interpretation have much that we may draw upon as we seek new ways to enrich our own dreams, our understanding of them and our application of this understanding to our waking lives.

Kilton Stuart, a psychoanalytically trained anthropologist, has spent a great amount of time studying Senoi society and techniques for working with dreams. Under the influence of Stuart's love for them and their dream methodology, the Senoi may have idealized their dream reports and applications. Nevertheless, the ideas of the Senoi as Stuart reports them can contribute greatly to our understanding and use of our own dreams.

An important contribution of the Senoi is the high esteem they accord the deepest levels of the human unconscious. Stuart reports that the psychic and emotional health of each tribesperson is the first priority of life among the Senoi. From the time a child learns to talk, he is taught to tell his family about his dreams as soon as he wakes up. All of his dreams are accepted and applauded, no matter how frightening, murderous or grandiose they may be.

By looking at your dreams from a Senoi viewpoint, you can strengthen your courage to explore yourself more deeply and to respect your dreams. You can learn to look at your own dreams through the eyes of an unconditionally accepted child who has not yet learned to judge or be judged and who looks at the world with infinite, insatiable curiosity. By starting on a dream journey with the Senoi, you can learn not only to bring some of your unconscious to conscious awareness, but also to have enough confidence to allow yourself to share your awareness with other people.

At breakfast one day, a little Senoi girl tells her parents her dream. With terror in her voice, she describes a nightmare about falling into a black, bottomless pit. Her parents tell her that she has had a wonderful dream, that to fall is to go far and fast and that not to know where she is going makes the possibilities of the dream rich. Next time she dreams that she falls she will be able to learn what the ability to move fast and to fly can give her. Her parents hint at great treasures to be found and brought back if she can stay with the fall and seek carefully. If she just lets herself go, allowing herself to be curious as she falls, how far will she go? To the center of the earth and through it? Out the other side? What stories she will be able to tell when she comes back!

A young boy of four wakes up screaming from a dream in which the fanged jaws of an enormous, roaring tiger are about to close around him. His family soothes him and then congratulates him on having had the dream. They gently suggest that, if he were to explore the giant white teeth, the gaping chasm that threatens to devour him, he might find a treasure. They wonder what a tiger would be like as a friend, or even a forcibly tamed enemy. They recommend calling in dream friends if he should decide he needs help to confront his foe. Above all, he is told not to flee or wake up from the dream. The tiger may, in the end, give him a present to bring back to his family or tribe. What might a tiger give as a gift? Perhaps a work of art, a dance, or a game that the child can produce and then present as his own gift to his family or tribe.

Frightening dreams such as these—one about the loss of control (falling), the other about being devoured—are universal. But these are only a few of the infinite variety of situations the Senoi learn to cope with in their dream lives. Just as the child is taught to approach fears in his dreams, he is also taught to approach pleasure or his own aggression in them, no matter how forbidden the object of desire or hostility may seem. It is critically important to Senoi dream work that the dreamer push his dream situation, no matter what it is or how forbidden the material it deals with, to resolution.

In the Senoi method, if the dreamer cannot meet the enemy or the object of desire in the dream, he must find some way to resolve the dream in fantasy or thought before he does the final dream work, the work that culminates in some form of socially valuable behavior. If damage has been done in the dream, it must be symbolically repaired *after* the dream has been worked through in thoughts and fantasies.

For example, the boy above may wish that universal wish—to get rid of his father and take complete and sole possession of his mother. He dreams that most common of dreams—that his father, a tiger, retaliates by eating him up or hurting him or maiming him in some sinister or violent way. The Senoi would instruct the boy to carry out aggressive and erotic wishes in dream or fantasy. The child allows the dream script to evolve until the crisis has been experienced and worked through. The crisis is reached at the point where the child decides either to wake up or run or, on the other hand, to work through a solution to his conflict. He might work it through by recognizing that the tiger represents retaliation by the father for aggressive and destructive feelings. To reach this recognition, the boy might be urged in his imagination or in another dream to enter into the jaws of the tiger. Once there he might explore the sharpness of the teeth, the wet roughness of the tongue, the warmth and smell of the tiger's breath, until he is able to become almost part of the tiger. In this way, he can possess some of the tiger's strength for himself. Or he might decide to fight the tiger, with the aid of helpers, if necessary. When he wins, he will again have gained some of the tiger's strength for himself. The ideal ending for this dream would be to overcome the tiger and then let it go.

In both cases, both tiger and boy emerge intact from the confrontation. The boy is a step closer to adulthood, where he gains strengths by identification with his father and by an enhanced and less ambivalent ability to compete healthily with father without destroying him. He will be more comfortable with his murderous wishes. As he becomes stronger, his horizons become broader and he no longer needs an exclusive relationship with his mother; he can permit her to have a relationship with the father, and the son can at least desire other relationships as well. He will eventually be drawn toward places outside his original family to fulfill his erotic and healthily aggressive, competitive drives. If all goes well, he will have learned to accept his fantasies, his murderous and incestuous wishes, and to relinquish murderous and incestuous actions.

How can we look at our dreams the way the Senoi do? The most important Senoi dream-viewing principle is to approach rather than avoid whatever you find in your dream. If what you find is ferocious or frighteningly attractive, you can call on allies to help you. Some people summon warriors to help them in their dream confrontation. Some use wise old men or women. Some use clever or vicious or beguiling animals to help them when they feel unable to face the dream enemy or to attract the dream object of desire alone. If you feel you need a helper and have difficulty in summoning one, then simply approach the difficulty itself. These sorts of difficulties are just as worthy of your attention as any other problems for which you seek resolution. They are just another danger to be approached and confronted.

A second suggestion, one useful for all finely honed listening and viewing, is to maintain as open a mind as possible, a state of innocence, as though you are seeing the world before you for the first time. You have just been born. You have no preconceptions. The dream unfolds before your freshly opened eyes.

After you have allowed your dream to unfold freely and have taken some time to explore its nooks and crannies, you may want to begin to integrate what you have learned into waking life.

As you follow along, you will probably need to turn back to my sample dream on page 27. Remember that all elements of a dream represent the dreamer more than any of the people, places or things dreamed about. In my dream, "I" am not limited to the character who has my name, face and body. I am also Barbara, Harold, Brazen Hussy, the timid Goody Two-Shoes and the other conferees, the dream itself; all are, in fact, projections of my mind. My identity even extends to the dream objects, things we consider inanimate in our waking lives: the objects in Barbara's purse, the assembly hall, the little pouches and their contents, the tote bag and the speakers' platform.

Before applying the Senoi methods to my sample dream, I thought about its setting again. In this dream, the setting provides me with a safe context in much the same way that Senoi society provides safety for its members to explore their dreams freely. The setting, the Berkshire Mountains, is the same as that of my high school. I was newly sprung from the rather repressive atmosphere of my family and my small Vermont town into a place where I felt free, accepted and frisky. It was the spring of my life, even though it is autumn in my dream. The dream setting tells me that I can still try on new characters and adventure creatively as I did then even though the dream, by taking place in autumn, questions how many full days are left.

Many people who work with dreams have used Senoi ideas to control the content of their dreams. I have found them more useful for understanding and approaching dreams that occur spontaneously. I like to use them to work toward resolution of my dreams in my thoughts and fantasies after I have awakened. However, if you are interested in taking some control of your dreams as you dream, follow this procedure:

At night as you go to sleep, chant to yourself soothingly and rhythmically a sort of lullaby suggesting over and over again that you will respond to the forces, characters and objects that appear in your dream in the following ways. You will:

1. approach and confront anything that seems dangerous, enlisting the aid of an ally, if necessary.
2. consummate pleasure with anything attractive.
3. find something in the dream to contribute to your waking life, and if possible, to your community.

If you can't accomplish all this while asleep, you can complete your dream work after you wake up. Proceed in a similar way with your waking fantasies.

This process is not the same as the process of dream incubation described in the previous chapter. In dream incubation the goal of the dreamer is to produce a dream solution to a specific problem or issue of waking life. The goal of a dreamer who uses the Senoi method is to achieve a harmonious balance between his unconscious self, his conscious self and his social unit by a process of integration of his dream life into his waking life. It is aimed more at acceptance of the dream, at nonavoidance, and at a positive regard for dreams regardless of content.

As I look at the structure of my dream and accept that all parts of the dream are parts of something that is happening within me, I will see that, although I didn't use Senoi techniques to control the dream, I handled both fear and longing as the Senoi do while I was dreaming. I confronted the fear, enlisting the aid of several helpers, and moved toward fulfillment of my wish. And I brought back a gift, the dream itself, to present to you, my readers.

For example, when I began with my first Senoi-type question, after establishing the tone of the dream's setting, I asked:

Q: *What is the fear in this dream? Who is the enemy?*
A: The first immediate enemy is the fear itself. I recognize my fear of speaking to large groups, which the large assembly hall represents. In this dream, there is no one on the speaker's platform, and I have the sense, as I answer these questions, that my fear is probably waiting for me there. Another fear is the thought of going into Barbara's purse and "stealing" something out of it, or nosing about in a place where I shouldn't be. Third, I am afraid that I will be caught doing it. Fourth, I am most afraid of what will happen if the contents of the bag are exposed. They clearly represent an unknown part of me that I am afraid might be too shameful to show to other people. Goody Two-Shoes, whose gasp has a moralistic sound, represents the frightened part of me.

Q: *What are the potential consequences? (In this dream, for example, if I speak, if I nose about, if I take something belonging to someone else, get caught or exposed, what might happen?)*
A: Disapproval, ostracism, being cut off, shame—all of these come to mind.

Q: *What pleasure do you want to fulfill in this dream?*
A: I want to satisfy my overwhelming curiosity. I have a powerful need to know what Barbara has.

Q: *How do you cope with the fear?*
A: The character of Margot (me) in the dream is paralyzed, unable to do anything to get what she needs. But, fortunately, other elements of the dream come to my aid. These emerge as the dream plot unfolds. My helpers are, first of all, the benign setting; Barbara, who says it's okay to show the hidden contents of our pouches to the world and laughs, helping me take myself less seriously (she also

doesn't even raise an eyebrow when Brazen Hussy invades her bag); Harold, who doesn't appear but also says it's okay; the people clustered in small groups who continue talking, more interested in each other than me; Brazen Hussy, who has no fear of anything.

Q: *How do you consummate pleasure and integrate or resolve conflicts, for example, the conflict between the desire to know and the prohibition against asking for or getting the wanted information?*

A: I become Brazen Hussy. I reach right into the purse, grab the pouches, rip them open and show everyone everything there is to see. I am fearless. I don't care what people think about me or do to me. I can confront the danger, and I can push right through to get what I want to satisfy my curiosity. Margot can pretend not to know Brazen Hussy, as she does. She keeps herself intact. She doesn't steal, or nose about or expose things, and still gets what she wants because Brazen Hussy acts for her. And surprisingly, no one except Margot seems to have a problem with it. Even Goody Two-Shoes is silenced.

Q: *What product or action can you carry from this dream into waking life?*

A: The dream tells me to:

1. go ahead with writing my book; it isn't so important that everyone like it,
2. consult Barbara,
3. get busy on a paper soon to be presented at a clinic conference.

49

The Senoi treatment of this dream has helped me to clarify and to face some important issues and fears—specifically, my fear of speaking to large groups, which writing a book in some ways resembles; it helps explain my reluctance to write and to speak to groups, and my fleeting sense that I have no business doing this kind of thing. I also have to speak at a staff conference in a few weeks. These are current issues in my life that the dream addresses by dealing with older, deeper issues.

Deeper vulnerabilities and foibles are exposed in this dream: my sensitivity to criticism and to injury of my pride; my feeling that I may be fraudulent, that what I present as mine may not really be my own, and that I will be exposed; my dishonesty, which refuses to take responsibility for my bold grabbiness; my cowardice and priggishness.

The dream also presents the healthily aggressive, honest, no-nonsense part of me, which protects and goes after what I need and want: the intellectual curiosity of Margot, the assertiveness of Brazen Hussy and the reassuring presence of Barbara.

Working with this dream has helped me harmonize these parts of myself. In turn, the new harmony has led to a clarification of what I want to write and how I want to put it together. Everyone in the dream except the cautious prig, Goody Two-Shoes, has given me the go-ahead. I need her, as well as the others, to provide the restraint I might otherwise lack. I even have authority in the highly discriminating person of Harold, who says, "Go ahead."

As I have used the Senoi method, it has dealt more with the action of the dream and the animate actors in it than with the inanimate objects that were prominent in the previous chapter. It is not necessary that the dream elements worked with be animate. A dream has intrinsic integrity and harmony. In your dream and interpretation, you may want to interweave human and nonhuman elements, either objects or ideas, until you find a place where you know they belong. You will pursue dead ends and need to retreat. If you find dangling parts, you will need to change your approach.

Allow yourself periods of feeling puzzled. Let the material lead you. Eventually, the elements will come together in a harmonious whole that will make perfect sense to you. When you recognize the relationship of your dream to its outcome—a creative production of some sort—you will be struck with an exhilarating sense of discovery. All the pieces will miraculously fit together to give you a profound feeling of satisfaction, clarity, conviction and energy to complete whatever task is before you.

Worksheet
Senoi

Your dream:
(If it's a new one, write it down.)

To help confront fears, dangers or desires met in dreams ask: *What or who was frightening or seemed dangerous? or was the object of desire?*

What was the quality of the fear or longing?

What was the quality of the feared or desired object or person?

In the dream, do you run away or wake up? If so, close your eyes now, relax and picture or feel the dream in your head. Spend some time with it, looking at all the elements with equal care, but eventually turn to the feared or desired object. Go toward it in your mind. Notice any changes in your feeling as approach it. [You can't change the dream now, but you can change your feelings about the feared object and you can change a future dream.]

What more have you learned about the feared or longed-for object in this new exploration?

Take some time to note qualities you now notice, or changes that occur as you explore.

Am I more or less afraid or desiring than I was before?

Of the same thing, or something different?

If what you fear or want is too shadowy to visualize, go into the shadows, look at the underside and other sides of the dream elements. If what you fear or crave is the setting or atmosphere of the dream and not any particular part of it, notice changes in your levels and kinds of fear or desire as you explore them.

When you reach a point where your feeling about the feared object, the longed-for object or the atmosphere of the dream changes, go on.

How does this situation, this object or person relate to my current waking life?

What can I bring back from this dream that will be useful to myself or to others? An idea? A solution to a problem? An interaction with a person? A poem or a picture? All of these?

CHAPTER III

Freud and the Royal Road to the Unconscious:
A Way of Insight into Hidden Wishes

If wishes were horses, then beggars would ride.
— Mother Goose

Would you like to understand yourself and your unconscious wishes better? To learn more about what really makes you tick? What moves you and what paralyzes you? How your inner conflicts and unconscious motives may influence your behavior or thinking? How you thought as a small child before you knew grown-up language or grown-up rules of logic? If you want deeper self-knowledge of this kind, then a psychoanalytic view of dreams may be enlightening for you. According to Sigmund Freud, when we dream, we think the way a small child or a psychotic person thinks. We also carry the primitive wishes of our early childhood with us into our adult dreams.

We all suffer from lapses of memory, slips of the tongue and other apparently bizarre mistakes from time to time. We do things it is not our conscious intent to do, and we leave undone things we profess to want to do. Before the turn of this century, such errors were usually considered just what they seemed at face value to be—failures to operate correctly according to our conscious, rational will. More serious failures were often attributed to weakness in willpower or morality, and less serious ones, such as slips of the tongue, to chance. People tried to strengthen or create the will to do the rationally right thing or

55

to reform their behavior. Yet they found themselves continuing to engage in behavior they considered wrong, harmful or destructive "despite their better selves," and despite mighty efforts at self-improvement. Freud discovered an explanation for these phenomena: powerful, unconscious counterforces that are at work in all of us. We push the knowledge of these forces out of our awareness by repression, denial or some other defense because they conflict with accepted social and moral codes of behavior and with our own self-concept. These forces, or drives, as Freud called them, are our erotic and aggressive urges, which we reject. Freud considered them infantile and said that we learn to abolish the very thought of them early in our lives.

The problem, according to Freud and other psychoanalysts, is that these drives cannot be destroyed. They don't disappear just because we want them to. They go underground where, at unexpected moments, they break through in behaviors that appear irrational or out of control. Freud believed that these behaviors are prompted by our unacceptable, unconscious wishes and that the more we bring these wishes into consciousness, the more we can bring the behaviors they prompt under rational control. To make the unconscious conscious and to know oneself are the primary goals of psychoanalysis. The "royal road" to this knowledge, according to Freud, is our dreams. The discovery of the unconscious was revolutionary to the Western world of the turn of the century. Since the Enlightenment of the eighteenth century, and especially after the advances of the Industrial Revolution, belief in the power of scientific and rational progress to improve the condition of mankind had been gaining ascendance, particularly in Europe. Rational thought appeared to answer all our problems. Freud's discovery of the unconscious demonstrated how "irrational" we really are and overturned the prevailing scientific optimism. Paradoxically, his discovery actually extended the sphere of rational and scientific control to encompass our irrational and unconscious experience.

For Freud, dreams are the foundation of the unconscious; at the same time, they provide much of the evidence that it exists. Originally, Freud worked with his own dreams, but eventually he studied those of his patients, too.

Freud believed that dream symbols are disguises for repressed material, our unconscious drives. Dreams contain outward, face-value meaning, called "manifest content," which hides covert erotic and aggressive wishes, called "latent content." When Freud began to look at his dreams, he free-associated in a structured way to the manifest content of the dream and the elements of the plot line in the order in which they occurred. Later, he abandoned the chronological structure and free-associated to any part of the dream as it floated through his conscious awareness. If you do this, you will find that after a while the latent, previously unconscious content of your dream will begin to emerge.

The dreamer conceals the latent content of the dream, in Freud's opinion, in order to remain asleep while experiencing the fulfillment of forbidden wishes and drives. These drives would shock the sleeper awake if they were presented in unconcealed form.

Three important ways in which dreams conceal and distort repressed material, according to Freud, are by (1) condensation, (2) displacement, and (3) secondary elaboration. A brief description of these devices will help you recognize some of the latent content hidden beneath the manifest content of your own dreams.

Condensation is a process of disguising a dreams's latent content by distilling it. Freud took the analogy from the physical sciences, where condensation is the process by which vapor reduces to become liquid; a substance changes its appearance, but not its essential identity, so much that it is unrecognizable to the uninitiated. The dream itself is a distillation of many parts of our life and many characters who have played roles in it. A dream is a much more compact, economical expression of a theme than we could possibly produce in waking life. Goody Two-Shoes is not only a part of me; she represents my mother's admonitions to me in my childhood to be well behaved, society's demand that I follow its behavioral prescriptions, and all the fundamentally self-righteous characters who have intimidated me since I investigated the bureau drawers of a great aunt I was visiting at the age of three and was slapped. Goody is a condensation of parts of my life since early childhood and many characters who have been important in it, including myself. In dreams one person, place, thing or situation condenses many others into a single representation.

Displacement conceals the latent meaning of a dream by giving weight or emotional value to the manifest content. The crucial, latent content is relegated to remote corners such as a minor character or an out-of-the way detail. Displacement can be compared to a magician's sleight-of-hand or to a more direct disguise such as a wolf in sheep's clothing, for example. The

devouring tiger in the boy's dream in the Senoi chapter is really his father in disguise. Without the disguise, the terror for the boy of being threatened by his father, whom he both loves and fears, would have been too painful to tolerate.

A clue that displacement is occurring is the bizarre appearance of someone or something in a place where the person or thing normally would not or could not be. Or, if most of the action that seems at first glance to be most important occurs on the left side of the dream scene, it may be that the crucial part of the dream happens on the right side. In my dream, the shapes in Barbara's bag are distinctly odd things to find there. It would have been easy to dismiss them because it isn't at all clear at first glance what they are. You will probably see examples of displacement in my dream that I have missed, perhaps a symbol that represents something painful or shameful. It cannot be denied, even by me, that the invasion of the pouches by Brazen Hussy is an expression of aggression and eroticism. The drives are undoubtedly my own, but the dream has displaced them onto Brazen Hussy, an apparently minor character.

Secondary elaboration disguises by filling in gaps with our rational functioning. We do this both while we are dreaming and when we remember our dream after we wake up. When we make logical sense of a dream, we cover up the mode of operation of the unconscious. One of the goals of free association is to avoid making logical sense of a dream prematurely. The need for rational comprehension is one of the forces that makes free association so difficult. When I follow the plot line, as I did in writing my dream, I may be hiding in secondary elaboration the fact that the aim of my dream was to allow me to indulge freely in violence and sexuality by disguising these behaviors as something else. Most of the dream and all of my analysis of it might be elaboration.

There are many other mechanisms of disguise. You probably have some that are peculiarly your own. You may dream the opposite of your true wish. Brazen Hussy's heedless courage gives the lie to my own cautious fearfulness. By letting her act for me I can say to myself virtuously, "I would *never* do such a thing." Yet it is I who send her into Barbara's bag. She is a disguise for me. If I had snatched the objects out of Barbara's purse myself, I might have been so horrified at my brashness that I would have awakened and abandoned my wish. You or a character in your dream may deny relationships that exist among dream elements or create relationships that don't exist. Goody Two-Shoes is in no way related to Brazen Hussy, but the very smugness of her certainty about their unrelatedness leads me to wonder if it may not be false. I don't like Goody Two-Shoes in the dream, but she stands for someone with moral standards so high that I might not dare admit my dislike for her in real life, or if she appeared undisguised in the dream, I might not be able to dislike her without waking up.

According to Freud, we will do anything to obfuscate the real meaning of a dream because the purpose of dreaming is precisely to disguise real meanings.

As I work with my dream, I will point out where I see that the dream uses devices of disguise. You may see things in my dream that I miss; disguising sometimes works so well that even when we study our dreams we fail to recognize some of the latent thoughts, fears and wishes they represent.

How do we gain access to the powerful unconscious forces that underlie our dreams and so learn to reckon with them? For Freud, the chosen way is by free association to the material of dreams.

"And what is that?" you might ask. To free-associate means to allow your thoughts to go wherever they will, letting them settle and flit without trying to make sense of them or control them. It means keeping a sort of free-floating attentiveness going. Although this may sound like relaxation, and in some ways it is, it can be very hard to do. It means letting the omnipotent mode of thinking flow. This is the mode you used when you were very young, before you knew the laws of cause and effect and the limitations of your mental powers, when some wishes could be transformed into horses you could ride and other wishes could destroy.

Sometimes lying on the grass watching the clouds float by or lying on the sand near the ocean can help you free-associate to a dream. Try to approximate as nearly as possible the feeling of a young child held completely comfortably and lovingly in its mother's arms, having just been fed and changed and loved, feeling completely fulfilled for the moment.

I have found a small, inexpensive, hand-held tape recorder helpful in the process of free-associating to dreams. A tape recorder is considerably less expensive than a psychoanalyst, who is, however, helpful at uncovering latent content, which, alone, we often repress. Psychoanalysis is a large commitment, however; it is usually undertaken to bring about serious changes in the self or to relieve symptoms or solve problems in life, a role this book is not meant to play. You can free-associate to your dreams into a tape recorder with abandon, and when you have gotten a little distance from the material, you can come back to it to see what you may be continuing to avoid. There will always be pockets of ignorance that only another person could see, but you will gain access to areas of yourself that you didn't know existed.

Even without another person listening to you and even though consciously you don't want to, you will soon notice that you are censoring the material. If you find yourself intensely involved with one part of the dream, you may be censoring another part of it. Sometimes a wave of boredom or a distinct distaste for working on a distracting part of a dream means that you are trying to skip over something of importance. A sudden craving may arise for a cigarette, a snack, a drink or even to exercise or telephone a friend. It helps to note the digression and what was happening when it occurred. Do not berate yourself, but simply note the digression on the tape. It probably means that you are disguising material that you would rather not know about. When you go back, you will probably be able to see more easily some of the material that you wanted to avoid. You don't have to work on everything right now. You can go back to it later, when it reemerges, which it almost certainly will do, either in another dream or as you explore this one. Often your ability to penetrate the disguise is strengthened when you recognize the resistance that is holding you back.

Don't try to be orderly when you first record or when you

free-associate to the material. Lie in the most comfortable place possible. Give yourself a relaxed hour or so. When you have finished the hour, put the tape aside for a few days and then listen to it. Notice which parts of the dream you dealt with and which you avoided. If someone or something appears on the right side of your dream scene, ask yourself what was on the left. If a number or a date comes up, look at it with open interest. Ask in what ways it is familiar to you. What thoughts or feelings come to mind?

After you have finished this process (some dreams are so interesting that the process takes years) you may ask yourself interpretive questions. These are questions that relate to what you have uncovered in yourself, questions that pierce the very fabric of your conscious life and link the past and present of your work and love relationships. You will usually find that a recent event has tapped into a childhood memory to help uncover some heretofore hidden wish.

To apply this approach to my sample dream, I must abandon the question-and-answer interior interview method. If I had followed a pure Freudian approach from the beginning, I would not have incubated the dream or written it down as I did. Dreaming is primarily a visual experience. Putting a visual experience into words removes it from the original. Writing down the words further distorts the dream. A tape recorder can provide a means of bypassing what we lose in translation

when we write down our dreams. When we talk into a recorder or to another person, we usually describe more closely and immediately what the dreaming experience was than we do when we write. With a recorder we can approximate more closely the freedom of the associations we might make while lying on a good analyst's couch.

I begin by free-associating to the dream with as open a mind as possible. I am lying comfortably, my cat purring next to me, with a small, hand-held tape recorder. I have turned off the ring on my telephone and have set aside some time to spend with my dream.

The following is a somewhat shortened and edited version of my free association. It is interspersed with comments on some of the examples of disguise that I found upon listening to my tape recording several days later. The work of asking questions and interpreting was started several days after that and has extended over a period of two or three weeks.

I'm struck by the fear in the dream, a fear that runs like, "What would people say if they knew?" The visual part that I see is the platform. What would people say if I performed? The platform is for teaching or learning, a very public place, but this reminds me of the very private place in me that's hidden.

Notice the use of opposites here. In waking life the platform functions as an open place for public activity, but when I free-associate to it, it reminds me of a closed place for private activity. My fear of performing is a fear of revealing what I want to keep private.

[At this point, the cat meowed, and my association shifted to the pouch, the rubber thing.] I'm just going to see what it's like, what it means. It's expandable, like a womb, which is also contractible. I think of just the word womb and how it sounds, *womb, womb, womb.* The place where things grow, where a lot of important things happen, a very protected place, *womb, womb.* A womb is like a room. It protects you.

And what is inside this womb-room? There are all of these shapes, these different functions, the triangle, the chess pawn. A cylinder—now, that is a more satisfying and stronger object. That stands up straight. A cylinder, a cone, a pointed cone. These are all the basic geometrical shapes. They're like something rational. And this complicated network of membranes leads to them and holds them together. The rational part is these pure geometric shapes. I would have expected something more organic, living, not something that seems to be made of some hard, nonliving substance made in a laboratory, not grown. These things may even be made of plastic. They're hard, rational. So maybe this irrational, amorphous, soft, expandable womb has a hard edge. But it's hidden. And if I were to stand up on that platform? Ohhhh! All the insides would come out for everyone to see. I and my usually hidden parts might be attacked for being grown-up. Grown-up means uppity and prideful and superior. You hurt people and then they want to hurt you. Grown-up also means taking over your mother's place in the world, including her sexual place.

We see here some condensation of opposites into one; the hard, strong, plastic shapes are joined by soft, delicate tendrils; the elasticity, expansiveness and protectiveness of the pouch hides the brittle, hard, intrusive plastic shapes. The brittle plastic substance has been displaced into an otherwise soft fecundity. However, as I go along with the free association, the pairs that seemed incompatible start to come together in a sort of mating.

The dream begins to take on an extremely sexual male-female feeling here. [The hard, plastic shapes seem to represent masculine power, aggression and intrusiveness, while the soft, pliable pouch and tendrils seem to represent encompassing, yielding feminine qualities.] Their joining together is clearly a sexual joining, but the sexuality is forbidden because it is competitive and exhibitionistic. If it were known, it would endanger me. This is really turning

out to be a very good Oedipal dream. It's a sort of if-I-per-
form-in-public, if-I-get-to-be-the-one-in-front kind of
dream. I think of Joseph's dream about the sheaves of
wheat. One of the sheaves stands upright and the others
bend over to it. When Joseph tells his brothers about his
dream, they want to kill him. They put him in the pit with
the lion. [I have condensed Joseph and Daniel in my associations to the dream.] That's very dangerous. Yes, that
might happen to me. This dream might too grandiose, or
the sexuality in the dream might be too grandiose. So I'm
letting Brazen Hussy do my dirty work, pretending she's
not me and pretending it is Barbara and not me who has
both the pouch and the little sacs. [Displacement occurs
when Brazen Hussy, not me, carries out my wish.]

As I free-associate to this material, the opposites begin to
take on an integration, like the pairing of male and female. The
hard and soft dream elements begin to penetrate each other,
and this is frightening to me. It seems as if I might take my
place on the platform to become an adult with the sexual impli-
cations of adulthood, but a conflict arises in me and I am afraid.
I think of the Oedipal conflict that Freud used to explain one
of the most important developmental passages from childhood
to adulthood.

Freud's theory of the Oedipal conflict was pivotal to his
thinking and deserves a brief digression here. In the Greek
myth, because of an oracular prophecy that Oedipus would
grow up to kill his father and marry his mother, the child was
given to a shepherd, who was instructed to leave him on a
mountainside to die. The shepherd instead sent Oedipus to a
family in a distant city to be reared as their own child. Learning
the prophecy about himself from another oracle, Oedipus left
what he thought was his family but met his true father, whom
he didn't recognize, on a highway, had an altercation with him
and killed him. Then, by solving the riddle of the Sphinx, he
won in marriage the woman who, though he didn't know it,
was his mother. So the prophecy was fulfilled, with disastrous
results. Freud saw in this myth the shadow of our universal

desire to possess our opposite-sex parent, a desire that implies the wish to destroy the other parent. Until we relinquish our incestuous wish, we are caught in childhood, unable to perform sexually or professionally without conflict, or to deal easily with authority when it reminds us of our hated parent. The Oedipal conflict plays itself out in the fear of growing up and taking on the tasks and responsibilities of adulthood—professional, sexual, and in relationship to authority and responsibility. The erotic and hostile emotions associated with Oedipal conflict go underground into the unconscious, to be found in unexpected places, in lapses at work, in sudden irrational fears and in various other blocks to competence, creativity and intimate relationships, particularly sexual ones. An important reason for these blocks is fear of retaliation from our same-sex parent. (In the chapter on the Senoi approach to dreams, the boy who dreamed that a tiger was threatening him was experiencing an Oedipal conflict.)

In my dream we begin to see fears of assertiveness, competence, and taking my place in the world. These are types of fears that I associate with Oedipal conflict. The free-association passage I've just given tends to corroborate this. The cost to me of joining elements thought to be unjoinable, which involves both competition and exhibitionism, might be that someone will try to kill me as Joseph's brothers tried to kill him when he, the youngest of them, told them he was destined to be their leader. Joseph's brothers are possible displacements of my mother, who, in my unconscious drama, I believe might want to kill me because I want to get rid of her. They might represent siblings, but this possibility didn't suggest itself to me when I explored the dream.

Another example of displacement in the dream involves the actions and characters of Brazen Hussy and Goody Two-Shoes. I displace my own wishes to see and display the secret contents of Barbara's bag onto Brazen Hussy. Goody Two-Shoes permits me to carry out the displaced voyeuristic and exhibitionistic wishes by denying that she has anything to do with it. "I would never go into Barbara's purse," she says. And, "People aren't allowed to know about these things." I must not look at the contents of the purses of others and I mustn't display the contents of my own. But in the dream, I do look at the contents of Barbara's purse by allowing Brazen Hussy to fulfill the wish. Goody Two-Shoes helps me retain my virtue by denying that I would ever do such a thing. There is a second displacement here in that I give Barbara the ownership of the bag, though it really belongs to me.

You can let your dream take you where it will as you follow your free-floating awareness along. Forget my sample dream when you do it. Relinquish any expectation of what you will get from your dream. Try not to impose any ideas on it, but let the dream lead you. Then, when you have spent some time free-associating to your dream over a few days, you can ask the following questions about the dream itself and the material that was uncovered when you free-associated to it:

1. What triggered this dream? What happened to me on the day of the dream or the day before that resonated in my unconscious so that I chose to dream of it?
2. What does the dream, or elements of the dream, remind me of from the past?
3. How do these elements relate to the triggering events or to what is going on in my life now?

My need for dream material for my book triggered this dream. Incubating it sullied its spontaneity a little, but since it produced rewarding material, I'm using it anyway, with some reservations. When you look at a dream in a Freudian way, it is better to use a dream that arises without direction from you.

Another trigger for my dream was talking to a friend the day before about my upcoming presentation on dreams to a professional group and wondering whether I can use material from the book in my presentation. Your dream will have several triggers as well. Spontaneous dream triggers often have little or nothing to do with the meaning or import of a dream.

After you have answered the first question, you can use both the dream content and the associated material to answer the second and third. The answers to the three questions may then be analyzed. A successful dream analysis links memories from the past with what is happening now and how the dreamer feels about it. The dreamer learns something about how his past is influencing his present. In my dream I was reminded of some of my ancient childhood conflicts. Several are in the dream, but most prominent is the old belief that if I should take center stage, or go for what I want, I would lose all my ties of affection to other people. They might disapprove of me, be envious of me or be afraid of me. This fear is related to the fear of making my mother angry. Being able to look more clearly at this conflict doesn't necessarily resolve it, but knowing that it is there and what it is about frees me to go on with my writing and my presentation. Even though some of the self-knowledge uncovered is painful, gaining new insight has a freeing effect. It will have a similar effect on you as well.

A word of caution when you use Freudian methods to analyze dreams: if the material is too painful or seems dangerous, you can stop or proceed more slowly and delve less deeply. You may decide to find a professional to help you work through the material.

Worksheet
Freud

Record your dream, on tape, in writing or in your memory, including any associations that float into your mind. Do this while lying down or sitting quietly relaxed.

Your dream:

When you have recorded the dream and your associations to it, set the recording aside. In a few days, come back to the material and ask:

What triggered this dream?

What do the elements of the dream remind me of?

Do you recognize any examples of
  Condensation?

Displacement?

Secondary elaboration?

Other forms of disguise?

What strong wish (or wishes) is expressed in the dream?

How do past events relate to your dream and to the triggering event?

How does your dream relate to what is going on in your life now?

CHAPTER IV

Jung's Approach to Dreams:
A Way to Synthesis

To use your dreams to enhance your spiritual development; to more deeply realize the shared universe of all humankind; to recognize universal symbols (archetypes) and feel a oneness with them; to analyze and familiarize yourself with the characters and figures (shadows) in your dreams, those parts of yourself that you deny in order to preserve the self you like best, your persona, and show it to others so they might like you, too; to move toward a synthesis, not just of yourself but of all humanity, a merging of heretofore hidden parts of yourself with a universal unconscious, these are some of the goals to which Jungian dream work is directed.

To Jung, an early and close disciple of Freud's, dreams represent elements of both a personal and a universal unconscious. He parted with Freud bitterly, because he disagreed with Freud's emphasis in psychoanalysis and dream interpretation on incestuous, sexual wishes. Although he rebelled, he retained, probably unknowingly, the basic structure of Freud's theories and goals, the assumption that psychic healing consists of making the unconscious conscious. He deemphasized the role of unconscious sexuality and aggression that we find in Freudian theory. To Jung, knowledge of our unconscious can be a source of spiritual and psychological wholeness or integration. Where Freud analyzes, Jung tends to synthesize.

Jung's treatment of dreams differed from Freud's in several ways. He did not differentiate as Freud did, between manifest and latent content of dreams. He treated objects and characters in dreams as overt representations of parts or dynamics of the dreamer's or all mankind's psyche. Because they are not bound by rationality and logic, or by space and time, dreams use a symbolic language to present a great amount of material on many levels in a few minutes. Moreover, according to Jung, the symbols do not necessarily represent conflict arising from infantile wishes and drives, as Freud believed; they stand for a broad range of both individual and universal human experience, from contemporary time to the beginning of mankind. To Jung, dreams reflect the individual's personality structure and place in the human spiritual and mythological universe. To understand dreams gives a person a sense of wholeness and of belonging to the family of man and God. Dreams often link us to some presence larger than ourself.

The theoretical concepts that are important in Jungian dream work are, on an individual level, the persona and the shadow. On a universal level, they are the archetype, the anima or animus and the map of the ground that contains the dream and the life drama, the mandala.

Our *persona* is the face that we prepare to meet the world with. It is ourself as we would like to be known or seen and, as time goes on, as we begin to see ourselves. Because I am female, I probably carry a persona that has more femininity than masculinity in it, according to whatever these terms mean to me. I may believe that it is bad for a woman to be assertive and that I should serve the emotional needs of others at the expense of my more assertive and demanding self.

Our *shadow* is the darker, underlying part of ourselves that we often don't recognize, except in dreams or involuntary behaviors. If I see myself as a gentle woman and I dream about an Amazonian woman who goes to war and behaves violently, the dream is a clue that I am denying my more hostile, aggressive shadow. My self that has too long served others at my own expense might appear in a dream as a squalling brat of a needy female baby, or as a ruthless snatcher like the Brazen Hussy in my dream, who takes what she wants no matter how many people she tramples on. These characters, the Amazon and the needy baby, and also the Brazen Hussy in my dream, are my shadows. Shadows show up as the opposites or negatives of the qualities we claim for ourselves.

The second three terms describe the collective, or universal, unconscious. They are the archetype, the anima or animus, and the mandala. Jung sees these elements depicted in important dreams that tap into our mystically shared humanity.

The *collective* or *universal unconscious* is partly and roughly the part of our psyche that gives us a shared sense of belonging to the family of man. It consists of the deeper parts of our psychological makeup that are common to all mankind. Tapping into it gives us a feeling of participating in history and sharing the deeper aspects of existence with all humanity. The best access to the collective unconscious is through our dreams, but myth, fairy tales, and religion are other expressions of it.

Dreams that emanate from the collective unconscious are inhabited by *archetypes,* among whom are the *anima* (if you are a man) and the *animus* (if you are a woman). If we study these dream elements over a period of time, they present themselves in configurations that seek to form a *mandala.*

An *archetype* is an image that we find universally in dreams. Just as all human bodies are endowed with two arms, two legs, a body, a head and other characteristics that define them as human, all human psyches are endowed with archetypes, the basic, universal and defining parts of the human psyche. According to Jung, who studied many of the world's religions and mythologies in depth, archetypes transcend culture. They appear in the dreams of Bushmen in Africa and of nuclear scientists in Los Alamos. They recur and become prominent themes in a series of dreams. You may recognize one because it feels especially important to you, or because it shows up in your dreams as a cultural symbol, such as an eagle, a witch, a wise old man or some other fairy tale, biblical or religious character or symbol. It often inspires awe in the dreamer.

A character in a dream who represents an archetype is called an anima or an animus. It is a character of the opposite sex from the dreamer. The anima, if you are male, or animus, if you are female, according to Jung, is usually someone whom you have never met in waking life and who is often quite unfamiliar in other ways. It doesn't need to be human. The unknown in a dream represents an unknown part of your unconscious. It is often a figure from the universal unconscious, the source of fairy tales, myths, religious and mystical symbols as well as of dreams. The anima or animus may be thought of as a special case of the shadow; embodying the reverse of one's sexual type, it is the feminine part of a masculine personality and the masculine part of a feminine personality. To become familiar with it helps us embrace the opposing and contradictory forces of existence.

The *mandala* is a cosmic diagram based on our world view and our view of ourselves in the world. Every person's mandala is different, and it changes during a lifetime. Completed mandalas share certain qualities such as symmetry and order, but their content varies with each individual and each culture. Jung found many shared qualities in the mythologies of the world and in dreams and religious symbols everywhere. The Star of David and the Christian cross are examples of mandalas. While an archetype is an object or character of the universal psyche, the mandala is the stage on which archetypes play out their cosmic action. It is the opposite of chaos. When a dream diagram produces a symmetrical, balanced and orderly composition, the mandala has been completed, and the dreamer has synthesized and integrated elements of his personal psyche and the universal unconscious. He has given order to the chaos that threatens us all and has achieved wholeness for the moment.

According to Jung, dreams appear in a thematic series. A single dream is inadequate to the task of understanding. Subsequent dreams clarify the issues. Our dreams tend to repeat themes until they are adequately understood and integrated. My Jungian work on my dream is only a beginning,

and it can show only a few of the possible ways to begin
Jungian work on your current dream. It substantiates some of
my earlier conclusions about my dream. Subsequent dreams
have sullied the purity of my treatment of the dream, but the
techniques of dream investigation still hold and can be helpful.

A Jungian technique that Fritz Perls later developed more
highly in Gestalt dream work is to carry on an interior dialogue with dream elements or characters. This technique is
elaborated in the following chapter.

One goal of Jungian dream work is to synthesize the dream
elements into a unified, but not a rigid, whole. One way of
working toward this is by drawing or painting a dream.
Drawing a dream helps us to learn to include our shadows as
we recognize them and defines more clearly both our individ-
uality and our collective universal qualities. We emerge with an
awareness of our concept of our world and ourself in it. We can
symbolize this process by integrating various elements that
appear in our dream into mandala formations.

Because Jungian theory emphasizes visual experience, I
decided to draw my dream, not artistically, but just to get a
sense of the relationship of the dream elements to each other.
I made a sort of a map or chart showing distances, relative
sizes, and relationships of the dream elements to each other. As
I drew, I recorded a running verbal commentary on tape. Part
of that commentary follows.

You, too, can make a diagram of your dream and look at the
relationships in it. As you draw it, note the feelings and
thoughts that arise. If you are uncomfortable with drawing,
you can make the pictures mentally by visualizing. The process
of acquiring new knowledge about yourself as you draw can be
quite exciting. Let the pencil or crayon freely follow your associations. You need not be limited by the dream text. Jungian
work seeks to transcend your personal text and find universals.

When I begin to draw my sample dream, I start by drawing
the circular tiers of seats in the lecture hall, so that I have ten
concentric circles. I begin almost to let the circles draw themselves, thinking smugly, "Look, here's a mandala already." It is
beautifully symmetrical. It is orderly. It is even in the shape of

a planet and seems to be becoming a representation of an orderly and predictable cosmos. However, after a few smug minutes, I notice that the circles are broken by the speaker's large, high, rectangular platform. Just as I achieve peace and effortlessness in this microcosmos, I realize that the mandala is incomplete in the area of the platform. I have more work to do. I'm struck by the emptiness of the platform and the round center floor of the auditorium. I also feel an enormous sense of how much I don't know as I look at my drawing. After experiencing these empty spaces, I discover that beyond their emptiness, they possess virtues of neatness, order, and clarity of outline. I feel curious about what might happen here.

I then begin to sketch Barbara, me and know-it-all Goody Two-Shoes in our seats. However, the drawing is too small to show the women's physical differences or the totebag in the context of the larger amphitheater. I get a sense of the minuteness of the principal actors in this enormous context. Our little drama may not have great importance in the universe. My free associations (or possibly an avoidance of the emptiness of the platform or the conflict between the women) move me outside the amphitheater to the surrounding mountains. Since the Jungian approach allows us to seek our place in the larger universe, I let myself be carried away from the original dream text into increasingly larger surroundings. I move into the landscape and I find that our theater is nestled in a bowl-like valley in the mountains, protected by smallish pine trees and a bubbling brook.

As my pencil moves farther afield, the trees become larger, then stop. They give way to huge, snow-covered, craggy wildness and the sky beyond it. These are no longer the Berkshire mountains, but mountains that have evolved from my dream. (If you are following by sketching a dream, you don't need to be bound by what was actually in the dream.) Although beautiful, my new mountains are definitely dangerous. I think of landslides, death by freezing, falls into chasms and various horrors of the unknown outside the sheltered bowl valley and the amphitheater. We are barely visible in comparison to the vastness around us. I have a sense of being one of the tiny figures in a Chinese landscape, going about my daily tasks amid cosmic happenings, hauling my water, chopping my wood, now neither endangered nor unendangered. I see that I am carried far away from the boundaries of my dream.

I continue drawing the setting of my dream, elaborating and enriching it with words and altogether enjoying the experience, as you probably will, too. However, the limitations of space and patience of the readers require that I go on to work with the characters in the dream.

My telescopic lens zooms in on the three of us, Goody Two-Shoes, Barbara and me as we sit in the amphitheater. I draw the chairs, which I realize for the first time are identical. I am surprised that three people sitting in the same room in identical chairs can be having such profoundly different experiences. I begin to draw the figures in the chairs. Barbara is very tall. She and her bag, in front of her and to her left, make a sort of protective semicircle around me. Goody Two-Shoes is leaning over me, straight and tense. Her nose is long and sharp, and all of her jagged edges point at me. She is mean and, above all, alert. She doesn't want either Barbara or me to have anything nice, especially me. When I draw the picture I see that she is so pushy in the space she takes up that she makes me feel rebellious and thereby pushes me into the very pleasure that she doesn't want me to have. The real central character is the tote bag. There it sits, compositionally the center of this group. The group is frozen here. There is a stalemate in the war between the wish and the prohibition. Barbara represents the moderate force, but she doesn't break the tense stalemate that we are locked into. The tension breaks only when the Brazen Hussy swoops down. As I draw her, she becomes a bird of prey, a huge-winged eagle whose talons and beak zero in on the two little pouches. There is a ruthlessness about her. As soon as she has opened the bag and the pouches, the tension in the circle of people evaporates. Goody Two-Shoes gasps, but relaxes. The worst imaginable disaster has happened to her and she can now relax her vigilance.

Goody Two-Shoes, Brazen Hussy and Barbara are my shadows, and since Brazen Hussy becomes a swooping eagle, in Jungian terms she may also represent an archetype, a more universally shared version of a shadow figure. Your dream will have its own archetype or shadow, an animus or anima, possibly a guiding grandmother to help you in life, or a sinister witch or ogre, a challenge for you to include in your internal cast of characters. When I had worked some more with these characters, I went to the contents of the little sacks.

As I draw the ganglia, they join together at the center, something like the body of an octopus, but with less substance. The slim, wispy tentacles reach, and indeed grasp, the geometrically shaped objects, but it seems as I draw that I want to go back to find a center, a firmer connection to the nucleus of the wispy ganglia, a central locus that connects the forms with each other. Otherwise, I am in danger of losing all connection. I think of Yeats's, "Things fall apart, the center cannot hold." I need to look at the way I connect things rather than to find more things to connect as I draw. The geometrical objects have less importance now, except as they need to be held together by the fragile tendrils. As I work with the dream, it becomes helpful in looking at what is happening to me now as I try to tie up my chapters into cohesive wholes, something extremely difficult for me to do. Even though it was dreamed before the writing, the dream addressed a problem I have with pulling in more material than the structure can support in a cohesive whole. Now it tells me to pay more attention to the supporting structure of myself and my book than to the objects the structure needs to hold together.

You can see that working on your dream in a Jungian way can lead you, too, to a synthesis of various strands of your life. This is just one dream. To do this approach justice you will need to follow a series of dreams. In my dream many questions are left unanswered. The platform is empty. This mandala has no center. Is this a problem? Who is the empty platform waiting for? The ganglia reach out and grab things though they have no strength in their center; Am I being inattentive to my core needs and grabbing for things in life randomly to try to cover my central fragility (wispiness)? These themes will recur until I come to an understanding and synthesis of them. Elements that seem to call for completion come up again and again in dreams in different disguises until a synthesis takes place. Even after a synthesis, they may reemerge at different stages to be rewoven into the fabric of one's life and universe. Here are my examples of some elements needing synthesis:

1. The circle mandala of the amphitheater is incomplete.
2. The characters of Goody Two-Shoes and the Eagle, also known as Brazen Hussy, still conflict.
3. The hard geometrical objects need to be synthesized with the soft, wispy ganglia to give the ganglia hardness and shape, the geometrical objects softness and flexibility. A synthesis might help combine the contrasts into working

wholes. It is possible, however, that these elements have been synthesized by being held together in the tote bag.

4. The central point of this dream is still not clear. Is it the empty platform, the stuffed tote bag, the absence of a nucleus for the ganglia or somewhere else entirely?

Three syntheses that were expressed in the dream were:

1. myself and other humans in the universe (my "Chinese landscape" experience),
2. experiencing myself as both alike and different from others (the chairs being alike while their occupants' experiences of reality are profoundly different),
3. the envious voyeuse and the show-off exhibitionist in myself--the coexistence of these personalities no longer seems impossible. I can both watch others perform and take center stage myself. It is no longer a matter of one or the other.

In practical terms, work on the dream helps me to see the need for working on both myself and my book with more attention to cohesive wholeness than to details, or rare little bits of knowledge. We don't know what your dream will tell you, but there is great opportunity in the Jungian approach for adventure, beauty and creativity in coherent form. Even more important than the dream itself is what you do with it.

If you have followed the book so far, you will see many similarities in goals between the problem-solving, the Senoi, the Freudian, and the Jungian approaches to dreams, but with different emphases and different techniques. All the methods are powerfully psychoanalytically informed, even the Senoi, because our information about them came through the channel of a psychoanalytic anthropologist. This will be true of all the other methods we see as well.

Worksheet
Jung

Your dream:

What are the main objects, human and nonhuman, in the dream?

What is their constellation (their relationship to you and to each other)?

Who are the characters in the dream that you never saw before or who are completely unlike you?

What would life be like if you were that (or those) unfamiliar characters?

Do they have any qualities that are like you? If not, can you experience how they might be experiencing life in this dream? (Take special time for this.)

Is there any part of this dream that you would hate to be like?

When you find the part you would hate to be like, act it as though you were like that. For example, I can imagine that I am the Brazen Hussy of my dream and can create her feelings and thoughts in myself.

Are there any awe-inspiring, larger-than-life characters in your dream? If there are, be quiet while picturing them and wonder what they might have to tell you. How do they fit into your universe?

What have you learned from your dream experience that applies to your waking life?

CHAPTER V

Gestalt:
A Way to Immediate Integration

T o learn how to acknowledge, take possession of and enjoy your dreams, not symbolically but by really experiencing them in waking life for their own intrinsic value; to learn how to carry on conversations and interact with previously denied or unknown parts of your psyche, as represented by dream creatures, human and nonhuman, animal, vegetable and mineral and the emotions, from sublime to despicable; to expand your awareness and sensitivity to include these disowned characteristics; to develop the ability to capture the immediacy and spontaneity of a young child; to learn to let your inner parts come to the surface, where you can embrace them and let go of them when they are ready to retreat, or be integrated, to be replaced by a new configuration, which in its turn, you can embrace and allow to fade into your ground of being again; to finish the unfinished business that impedes you in life so that you are free to move on; these are some of the goals of Gestalt.

Gestalt theory addresses present events that encompass our total range of perception and feeling as we experience them right now. What is happening now, both during the dream and when we reexperience the dream after waking up, is an event or the appearance of an element in our personality that has not been successfully synthesized or resolved; it plagues us, making freedom and lively spontaneity impossible. There it will remain, screaming in the foreground of our being or nagging us like a missing piece of a jigsaw puzzle, until we acknowledge it fully and integrate it successfully.

In Gestalt, the puzzle consists of different elements of our personalities—often disowned elements that we would like to pretend have nothing to do with us. Gestalt therapy aims to help us take full responsibility for and claim authorship of our actions and our feelings, even those we meet in our dreams. Fritz Perls, the father of Gestalt therapy, called the integration of these elements into the ongoing process of our lives "owning our disowned parts." Integration takes place when we carefully attend to what rises and emerges as foreground in our consciousness. We stay with whatever surfaces without trying to push it away or do something else. The attitude we take toward it is, "This is me. This is mine," no matter how much we wish it were not or how antithetical it seems to our cherished view of ourself. We continue to explore it until it recedes into the ground of our consciousness and a new element arises to take its place in the foreground. The new configuration that appears will, in its turn, recede to give place to still another one

when another unassimilated element claims the foreground of our consciousness. This process repeats itself as long as life and growth continue. Instead of permanent solutions, we find a continuing process of challenge and resolution. It is important to note, too, that while we experience life events in the present moment, the feelings they give rise to may be triggered by a memory, a premonition, a dream or a fantasy. We experience all the events that challenge our predominant configuration or Gestalt in the present no matter when or where the event, actual or fantasized, took or might take place.

Wolfgang Kohler developed Gestalt as a psychological theory in the nineteenth century. Fritz Perls further developed the theory into a method of psychotherapy. The philosophical and theoretical bases of the school are outside the scope of this book, except to note that they provide us with a framework and rationale for much exciting, immediate and lively experience. They can help us cut through a tendency to overintellectualize and move us in new directions. Two Gestalt techniques that can be applied to dreams are (1) owning your disowned parts and (2) the empty chair.

In practice, owning your disowned parts is playing the parts of all the elements in a dream as you become aware of them until you feel yourself to be each of those elements. They are then integrated into your whole psychological configuration to be used as sources of energy rather than debilitating and exhausting repressions. For example, a young woman dreams that she is at the wheel of a car. As she begins to try to drive, she realizes that the clutch doesn't engage, the gears don't shift, and the car runs as it will, out of her control. She tries desperately to manipulate the clutch with her hands. She doesn't seem to be able to connect with the engine, so the power can't be reached. She wakes up upset, with no resolution.

The young woman begins to work with this dream by sitting quietly and letting what seems most troublesome come into the foreground of her consciousness. It is the faulty clutch. By taking the role of the clutch, which can't engage with the engine, the source of the car's power, she comes to recognize and explore ways in which her energy is not available to help her engage fully in work and love. As she imagines herself actually being a failing clutch she feels her helplessness and her powerful need to engage. The state of the car and its parts represent the state of her self and her progress in various areas of life. Eventually, in dreams and in life, her clutch engages, she takes control of her previously disowned energy source and is able to use it to decide what work she wants to do, to enroll in graduate school to pursue that work and to enter into a committed relationship with and marry the man she loves. Until she mastered the clutch, brake and steering wheel of her energy, she felt threatened by loss of control. Until the faulty clutch had been examined, she was unable to reach and take possession of the source of power that she needed to engage in life fully. Examples of owning disowned parts abound in this dream exploration, but the most important is the dreamer's new access to the energy that the engine of the car represents.

The empty chair is a gestalt technique for recognizing projections, the characters and objects of dreams. The dreamer sits across from a chair that represents a character or an object in his dream and talks to him, her or it. He talks about how he feels about the projection, what he wants from it, and who or what it reminds him of. When he has finished talking to this projection, he changes chairs and, playing the role of the projection, talks to himself, represented by the empty chair. In the role of his projection, he talks about how it feels, what it wants from him, and whom he reminds it of. This will sound and feel silly when you begin to do it, but you will learn more about yourself if you go ahead with it anyway. If you can throw yourself into it wholeheartedly, you will have a lot of fun.

For example, in working with my dream, I put Barbara in the empty chair across from me and talk to her. It feels silly to me, but I do it anyway. I don't limit myself to what happened during the dream. I continue to develop the dream though I'm awake. What I say, after looking at Barbara and getting a sense of what it feels like to be with her in the amphitheater in the beginning of the dream, goes like this:

> Barbara, I like being here with you. You give me a sense that you are centered and serene. I admire you and feel nurtured when I'm with you. When you read to us, or talk, it feels like being read to when I was a little girl.
>
> But I'm also aware that you have something or some knowledge that I want. I want to know what it is. But somehow it seems forbidden to me. And it's something I can't ask about because of this woman who's always on my back. So I just sit here paralyzed, getting hungrier and hungrier to know what's in your bag. Each time I feel this hunger, the

Goody Two-Shoes monkey on my back says, "Don't ask," and I feel hungrier for what you have in there, but the hungrier I feel, the less able I am to ask for it. You just sit there, calm as can be.

Remarks to a dream character might go anywhere, but I learned new things about my conflicts from even this snatch. I learned more directly that I tend to deny my own self-soothing ability and, instead of experiencing that part of myself, depend on others like Barbara to provide consolation for me. Barbara seems to have sole possession of the knowledge that, in my unsoothed state, I think I need to get from her, ignorant of the fact that I have both self-soothing capabilities and access to the same knowledge that she has in her bag. What I think I want from Barbara is reassurance, which, Gestalt methods show me, I also have or can give to myself. When it is not forthcoming, what Goody Two-Shoes represents in me makes it difficult for me to ask for it, to get it for myself, or to recognize that I might already have it.

When you begin to talk to your dream character or object, let yourself go anywhere. You can have a tea party, a small-talk conversation or a heavy, deep confrontation.

I then shift chairs and play Barbara—my internal, dream picture of Barbara, not to be confused with the actual Barbara of real life.

I want you to do well and I want to help you. You can have anything in my bag, but I can't push it into your hand. I can't *make* you ask. I can only sit here waiting for you to make the move yourself. I'm not even sure that the tote bag belongs to me. But if I make you take it, it will be as though it belongs to me and won't be yours. I can support you for what you already have done, but not for things you haven't done yet. And by the time you do them, you won't even need my support.

I'm beginning to own the part of myself that can take what I need and do something for myself and for other people calmly.

91

I begin to feel stirrings of the qualities that my dream has attributed to Barbara in myself—serenity and competence among others. The contents of her bag become knowledge that can be shared without fear. They seem to relate to both the writing of the book and my presentation. I then shift back to playing myself:

> I see what you mean [I say to Barbara]. I've been feeling that I don't have any right to take perfectly available emotional and intellectual stimulation and support, support that doesn't have to be taken at all, support that is just available. I'm suddenly feeling much more comfortable and solid. I feel freer and lighter.

When a shift in feeling occurs, an about-face kind of shift, then a new integration has been made. When I started the exercise, I was feeling desperate and torn between the two forces of Goody Two-Shoes and Brazen Hussy. My desperation surfaced because nosy Goody Two-Shoes (who listened in on my dialogue with Barbara) was harassing me. I experienced her as threatening. It seemed as if I needed to do something almost criminal to get what I needed. The shift occurred with the realization that I don't have to do such extreme things, that what I need is as available, and as essential, as the air around me. I have integrated some of the strengths and the legitimacy of Barbara. This gives me a sort of unflappability when facing Goody Two-Shoes. Although she has not yet changed or been integrated, her voice and watchfulness are less able to threaten me. I will still have to take her role and play opposite her before I experience, understand and integrate my own self-righteous smugness.

This vignette is an example of owning several disowned parts or qualities of myself by using the empty chair technique. I experienced and understood the greed I felt when it seemed what I needed could neither be had nor asked for. With the understanding that what I needed could be taken, the greed, no longer insatiable, was transformed into usable, healthy appetite. As I worked on other parts of the dream, the predatory qualities of Brazen Hussy seemed more related to simple intellectual curiosity and no longer seemed so shameful. Barbara's serenity was easily owned because it was a part of me that I liked and wanted. The parts of yourself that you find in your dreams won't always be likable. The unlikable parts are more painful, but ultimately more rewarding to work with. The shift in perception that you experience with unlikable parts of yourself is more dramatic and more rewarding than the shift you experience when you work with likable parts.

When you practice the empty chair technique, you give the characters in your dreams different contexts and different meanings from those you began with. Sometimes the shift in ground gives you the feeling that you have just "gotten" a very funny joke, often one that includes a double meaning. In my dream, the joke on me was that I wanted something from the tote bag very badly. I agonized about not stealing something.

As I worked through the dream I realized that the contents of the bag and all the other parts of the dream already belonged to me. When I worked with the empty chair, I came to experience everything in my dream as my own. So what was the big fuss all about?

This technique offers lots of opportunities to have a good time. You can play all parts of the dream. It is particularly enriching to play the inanimate objects. [The next chapter includes an example of enacting an inanimate object in a dream dramatization.] This is an especially good way of working with waking fantasies as well as with dreams.

Worksheet
Gestalt

Your dream:

To begin, let your eye, emotions or intellect look at the dream. What seems most important? And what about this element is important? (Spend a few minutes focusing first on yourself, then on this most important element.)

Merge identities with the important element by saying to yourself: *As the element or person of importance, I feel (heavy, light, smelly or any other possibility suggested by the five senses plus the emotions). I am used for (include all possible uses—practical, impractical, fantastical):*

Gestalt

When you push being the important element to absurd
lengths, what shift takes place in your awareness of yourself?
Of the important element?

What is your relationship to each other now?

97

Now what happens when you take the least important element of the dream, or something that was forgotten earlier, and subject it to the same treatment?

CHAPTER VI

Body Techniques:
A Way of Experiencing Your Dream Physically

To experience your dream with all your senses, in your muscles, nerves, lungs; to deepen and intensify the dream theme; to gain fluidity of both emotional and physical movement from it—these are some of the things that using body techniques when you work with your dreams can help you do.

Alexander Lowen (*The Betrayal of the Body:* London, MacMillan, 1969) believes, as medical and psychological researchers increasingly believe today, that our bodies are the seat of our emotions. I think anyone who has watched the pure physicality of a small child's emotions would agree. Psychoanalytically trained, Lowen posited that we use parts of our bodies as instruments of repression, denial or other mechanisms of defense against unacceptable feelings. According to Lowen, each time we push an emotion out of our awareness, a part of us stiffens. Eventually our bodies develop rigid areas. We build a sort of "body armor" around and in ourselves to protect us from threats from both inside and out. This armor is important for defending us from devastating hurt or loss of control. But when we can't remove it in safe situations, we lose

our ability to fully experience our lives. Our emotions begin to be absorbed or deflected before we are even aware that they exist. We lose our ability to feel, to move easily and spontaneously, and we can even become physically vulnerable to disease. By going directly to the body to work with our tense, rigid areas, Lowen believed we could reach hidden material that would otherwise not be available to us, such as long repressed or long denied feelings. After fully experiencing the emotions we have been using energy to harbor in our bodies, we have access to more energy to use creatively and positively. We can adapt Lowen's ideas to our work with dreams.

In my practice, this means acting out the roles of the various elements in our dreams. The player interprets dream elements with whole-body action, position and sensation. It is like the Gestalt treatment of dreams in its immediacy and its ability to open the dreamer to new experience. But in body work with dreams, players move about the room, breathe, swing arms, kick, and generally participate in dream dramas with their whole bodies. They learn different ways of responding to and acting in the world. Afterward it is easier to recognize and pursue their own goals based on their lived experience and not on what others tell them they should do.

Taking my seed dream again; first I (and you, if you are following with a dream of your own) give myself some time to get into the dream physically. I sit quietly, eyes closed, until I can be there in it, and then begin to imagine what my body would have felt in the dream situation. My body actually begins to feel it after a while. I don't try to stop the sensations, but exaggerate them almost to the point of hurting or collapsing.

> I let myself experience sitting in the auditorium, feeling the seat of the chair, the breath of Goody Two-Shoes. She is afraid of everything, even afraid to breathe too hard over my shoulder. My body is tense. I want to do something, but I can't, even though it's within my reach. The conflict between wanting the objects in Barbara's bag and Goody Two-Shoes's prohibition paralyzes me. In fact, my body is constricted. My hands are tightly and safely in my pockets

so that I am not able to do the forbidden thing. And I am trying to make my body as small as possible, to disappear, especially my right hand, the one that's beside Barbara's bag. My right shoulder is extremely tense; it twitches. My left shoulder is a cold shoulder for Goody Two-Shoes. It turns away from her, not wanting to see or hear her warnings and commands. "You mustn't," I hear, and try to turn my back to her. As I experience this in my body, I exaggerate the bodily sensations. If I feel the tension in my right shoulder, the seat of the conflict, I tense it up even more. I discover an important way that I constrict not only my body, but an enormous amount of energy, and when I intensify the constriction, my muscles knot. In fact, the whole situation is quite agonizing and paralyzing for me. Eventually I tighten so hard that the tension is forced to break and give way to relaxation and near ecstatic relief. My shoulder feels freed. I breathe deeply, and I immediately find myself wanting to identify with Brazen Hussy. Although I think I am freed enough to take her role, when I try to act her part, I can't. My body won't do it. First I need to deal with wanting to avoid something.

You will find parts of your dream that you want to avoid, too. It is better to play the part of the avoidance itself first, before going into what it is you are trying to avoid. You will probably try, as I did, to avoid taking a role and reach a dead end because of your avoidance. Play the dead end itself.

In doing this exercise I discover how much I try to avoid and disown the priggish, self-righteous Goody Two-Shoes. I want to run away from her and pretend she doesn't exist. Recognizing and physically experiencing my repugnance for her frees me to at least contemplate taking her role. Although I'm still not enthusiastic, I decide to begin to play her. Let's see how it goes.

I sit watching Margot (now represented by an empty chair) and breathe in the character of Goody Two-Shoes. I feel the tense alertness in my body. I have to watch every move Margot makes, look her up and down to see if there's anything wrong with her. The muscles in the back of my neck are stiff from watching her so intently all the time. My eyes are screwed up and my arms go to my hips so that I can tower over her, threateningly. My breathing is heavy and angry, and I want to tell her what I think of her. But if I tell her, she'll know what's wrong with her and be able to correct it. Actually, I don't really know anything that's wrong with her, but if she knew this, I wouldn't be able to control her and stand over her in this powerful way. I realize that because I have to control her so hard, with every muscle and constant day-and-night tense alertness, I am as paralyzed as she is. We are locked together; I can't let her move and can't move myself because she might do something wrong if I relax for even an instant. By "wrong" I mean something out of my control. I can hardly breath and push through my near suffocation until I take great gulps of air. At last I can breathe, which she can't do. And the breath I breathe is fiery.

I now take the role of Brazen Hussy. Having worked through and let go of my paralyzed, conflicted role, I feel free, exhilarated and energetic.

My breathing is deep and firm; my voice is strong when I say, somewhat to my astonishment, "What Lola wants, Lola gets." I don't care about good manners and am untrammeled by social conventions. My body is free as a dancer's. My arms feel long enough to reach across the room, and my stride is like the seven-league stride of Puss-in-Boots. When I bend over to grab the pouch out of Barbara's purse, I use every cell in my body. I hold the pouch high in the air for all to see. My chest is inflated and I breathe what feels like pride and competence.

When you work physically with your dream, if you find yourself deadlocked, unable to play or feel a part, you can go to another part of the dream and then come back to the one you couldn't play. You needn't be limited to experiencing yourself as a human being. For example, I play the part of a pouch with a drawstring around my neck.

> I tighten my neck muscles (drawstring) until I am nearly choking. I feel like someone who is cut off at the neck. All of the rest of me is shoved down, and I am unable to speak, breathe or experience my lower regions. Mostly it feels like fear that something that shouldn't might get out. What that something is that I'm stuffed with I don't know. I imagine Miss Know-It-All pulling the string even tighter. Finally, when I feel almost apoplectic, Brazen Hussy swoops down to relieve this near-death suffocation and let out these important parts of me. What a relief! Physically, my neck and shoulders are floppily relaxed; my breathing is deep, and I experience my body all the way to my toes. I'm floppy after she takes the contents out, but floppy in a comfortable way. I'm so flexible that I don't feel emptiness or fear, just relief and a softness that contains and protects my insides.

103

Though the emphasis here is on body techniques, you may speak whenever you want to try out the timbre of your voice in a particular part. It's probably better not to get into volumes of talk, but talk, yell, shriek, moan, groan, laugh, whine or make whatever noise comes out, more to hear sound and feel sensation than to express meaning in words.

From working in this way I gained a feeling of power over my own actions and of what it is that separates me from the realization that I can be the mover of my own life. The tightness of the drawstring of the pouch helped me see that I need to work on loosening the tight, overprotective hold I maintain over myself from the neck down to free up the flow between head and heart. I learned more about the positive aspects of feeling empty and realized that fear of experiencing my emptiness had been one of the reasons for my stranglehold on myself. Knowing this gives me freedom to feel without fear; I don't have to spend so much energy protecting myself. I can be much more flexible than the mean part of me has let me realize.

This and the psychodramatic techniques presented in the next chapter are especially good for working with nightmares. A young mother who was in the process of separating from her husband dreamed repeatedly about a terrifying shark who menaced her. After she was able to play the shark, to experience her body in the water frightening people with her enormous teeth, she felt her mouth turn from gaping maw to benign dolphin smile and continued to experience herself swimming (now playfully) in the ocean carrying a passenger on her back. As her experience of the nightmare became more physical and less visual and verbal, she began to experience her own power, playful pleasure in her own body, and her ability and even desire to take care of her young daughter by herself.

When you feel, touch, taste, smell and yell your dream, you will make discoveries, too. They will not be the same as mine, but they will give you a sense of power over your own actions as you play the role of things that seemed out of control in your dream. This sense of power carries over into broad areas of your waking life.

Your dream:

After giving yourself time to experience what it is like for you to be in the dream itself, gradually begin to focus on one of the elements or characters until you become one with it.

What do I feel?

How do I move? breathe? perceive temperature? smell? taste?

Where are my pockets of tension? of relaxation?

When I intensify the tension to the breaking point, what happens?

When I relax to the point of near-death limpness, what happens?

When you actively move according to the will of the character you are playing, do you stretch? shrink? sigh? shout? yawn? yell? whine? bang? punch?

Whatever your character's body wills, do to the fullest extent. What happens?

What new facets of the character emerge as you play out the dream in the flesh?

How can you integrate this character into your own?

Dream Theater:
A Way of Sharing Your Dream with Others

*I do not know whether I was then a man
dreaming I was a butterfly, or whether I am now
a butterfuly dreaming I am a man.*

– Chuang Tzu

To make a dream a shared experience; to create drama of your dream; to elaborate upon, broaden and intensify your experience; to resolve an unfinished dream or find a better resolution to an unsatisfactory dream; to make the dream happen here and now with real actors and actresses under your direction; to benefit from the insight someone else can bring to your dream; to elaborate upon or change your dream script so that you can make changes in your life—these are some of the goals of dream theater, sociodrama or psychodrama.

In Vienna in the 1920s, using the theater as his inspiration, J. L. Moreno developed a method of group therapy that he called psychodrama. He believed we all play out a "life script" based on early experience that we have internalized so thoroughly that we don't know it exists. We reenact our script over and over again throughout our lives. It is based on our interactions with people we knew and depended on when we were very young. But interactions modeled on earlier relationships are highly inappropriate now. Unfortunately, unless we become consciously aware of what we are doing, we don't know who is running our show. Is it ourself in the present, or our internalized cast of characters from the past who motivate us and control our behavior? Our efforts to change, to love or be loved by another person, tend to fail in the same way no matter what our conscious wishes to the contrary may be.

Dream theater gives us a chance to change the script by casting others in the roles of ourselves and our internal cast of characters. We can then redirect our own drama. Dreams represent a splendid opportunity to externalize and make conscious our self-defeating behaviors and reactions. By resolving unresolved dream plots, by elaborating on them in various ways, or by changing them completely, we can begin to change the life script that repeatedly rules and stereotypes our actions and interactions.

Moreno, using an actual stage in a theater, helped his clients to direct their life scripts. People from the audience were cast in the roles of characters representing aspects of the dreamer in the drama. Moreno called the consciously functioning ego of the dreamer the "protagonist." According to psychodramatic and other theory, our ego is the consciously functioning executive in us, the part of us that sees to our general welfare and our conscious activity in the world. It also mediates between our conscience and our forbidden drives and wishes. In Moreno's drama, the protagonist is the hero, the director and the main character of the dream as it is dramatized. He shares the stage with auxiliary egos, characters cast as his allies who can come to his aid or comment on or clarify the action like a Greek chorus.

But drama implies tension, and tension arises from conflict or contrast of character. In our drama there will be an antagonist, a villain whose wishes and behavior conflict with the conscious wishes of our hero, the dreamer. This villain can also enlist allies to come to his aid, and they are called "alter egos." They may represent a part of our hero that he is not consciously aware of, such as a forbidden wish, an internalized figure from his past or his usually more conscious, but despised, overly exacting conscience. All the figures on both sides, the good guys (auxiliary egos) and the bad guys (alter egos), the hero and the villain, represent parts of the dreamer's psychological makeup, whether he likes it or not. It is to the dreamer's great advantage to switch roles with some of the less savory characters in his dream. A villainous alter ego who seems completely foreign to the hero may prevent him from doing what he thinks he wants to do or what is good for him. This character may inhibit him in his efforts at intimacy or hinder him from tapping into his creativity. Once we know and understand these aspects of ourselves that are antagonistic to the functioning of our ego, their nature changes, just as other people do, or seem to do, as we get to know them better. In dream theater an enemy often is transformed into an adviser, a helper or a friend, like the mythical dragon who is conquered and tamed by the hero.

An auxiliary ego may be cast in a helping role, as a sort of Tonto to our Lone Ranger, or even possibly a double who can mirror our action so that we can see ourself from a new, broader or more objective perspective.

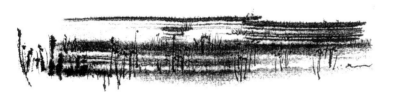

In psychodrama, we use a group of people to whom we assign the roles of our dream characters. We unknowingly assign these roles to others all our lives based on previous experience. A person who has been abused as a child sees violence and rage in others and unconsciously casts them in the role of abuser. The person behaves as if afraid without recognizing that there is usually nothing to be afraid of. However, the dreams of such a person are likely to show fearsome characters who, if cast and directed in a dramatic production of the dream, will begin to show new and different possibilities. This previously battered child can ask one of the members of his dream group to play the role of a child abuser or some other violent character, often an animal or a stranger, from the dream.

Now, in waking life, the dreamer can direct the drama as she couldn't in childhood or in repeated dreams of the childhood episode. She can come to understand that even though this one character is an abuser, others in the dream or in her life are not. Or perhaps by personally assuming the role of the abuser or paying close attention to the person acting that part, she may grow to understand the abuser's motivation and fragility and may experience a lessening of fear of that person. Such an understanding may enable her to gain more conscious control of what she does—her actions and reactions will become more reality-based and more flexible.

In a way, psychodrama is based on the concept of transference in Freudian psychoanalysis. It assumes that we behave toward others as we learned to behave in our earliest relationships. According to this theory, we transfer our early emotional and behavioral patterns onto our current relationships. We treat important figures in our lives now as we treated our loved or hated mother, father, brother or sister, or other people who were important in our early lives. These people or our images of them are now inside us, where they influence us and appear in our dreams, often disguised. We also tend to dream the same dreams over and over again until the issues they represent have been resolved. Making a dramatic production of our dream seeks to free us from repeating unrewarding patterns over and over again. It also gives us a euphoric feeling to experience ourselves as the actor and not the acted upon in life. We can rewrite our dream script and our life script. We feel the authors of ourselves and our actions.

To use this technique you need one other person or a small group of people whom you trust and who care about you, or you may participate in a group, usually of people previously unknown to you, with a professional leader to provide safety and to facilitate the drama. Once your actors begin to play their parts, they will gain much for themselves, even though they are playing parts in your dream. It is important to remember that the protagonist, the dreamer, is the director of the action at all times. She can stop it whenever she wishes, tone it down if it seems too intense, or recast right in the middle of the play. Any player can refuse a part or, if he feels he needs to, stop playing a part. It is better that the protagonist not cast members of her own family in a dream drama. Other people can play the protagonist at times so that the dreamer can play some of the auxiliary egos or alter egos. The protagonist, the principal character, is always the dreamer, no matter who is playing the part, but the true author of the dream is always the director. An alter ego, a villain, often is transformed as the action progresses into someone who can be used in the service of the protagonist. Other characters, whether in the actual dream or not, can be assigned to advise the protagonist, to comment on the action like a Greek chorus or to take more active roles in the play. Characters cast from dreams often represent the less conscious parts of the self or qualities of figures from the past. The protagonist can switch roles with these characters to his advantage.

113

Before staging a dream play, it is important to establish rules that make it safe for all the players to engage in the drama with as little fear and as much spontaneity as possible. The rules my small group used were:

1. Physical violence is forbidden.
2. The director or any other player may stop the action or change roles at any time.
3. What happens in our psychodrama setting is strictly confidential. There always needs to be some kind of rule about the level of confidentiality that the group wants to keep. [By unanimous consent, this rule was later waived so I could write about this meeting in the book. If there had been any opposition I would not have used it in my book.]

When your trusted group has gathered and has achieved a consensus on the rules it wants to follow, you are ready for the group warm-up. First, assess and articulate the mood of the group and each person in it until all feel ready to hear your dream and you feel ready to tell it. My group members felt shy, a little frightened and quite foolish in the beginning, even though we know each other well. I assured them that they wouldn't have to act if they didn't want to and that they could stop whenever they pleased. I knew they were safe from pressure when I let go of the pressure myself. I felt it go when I could say to myself, "I could easily find another group, or leave this chapter out of my book."

When your group is ready to hear the dream, give them as close an idea as you can of how it was for you to be in the dream and how it might have been for the other characters and objects.

When you stage your dream, gather your trusted group together. Relate the plot and the setting and describe the cast in full physical and emotional detail, demonstrating by gesture, voice, metaphor or any other device what you mean. Remember that you will be directing a play, and you want the players to have the fullest possible flavor of their parts. They should feel free to ask you to clarify. Let them talk about how they understand the dream. In this warm-up period, no one interprets or attaches meanings to the dream. Everyone just tries to learn and understand what happens and how the dreamer experiences it. Small groups are easier to manage in the beginning; I staged my sample dream with only two friends, Pat and Dorothy.

My group listened wide-eyed and rapt while I told my dream tale. I hammed it up, and I could see their bodies twitching. When I described Miss Know-It-All (Goody Two-Shoes), Pat said she knew *exactly* the kind of person I meant. Dorothy said, "I certainly don't want to play *her.* She's like parts of myself I don't like." They commented as I went along and as the dream spoke to them, becoming more and more involved. When they asked about the size of the hall, the fundamentals of the furnishings of the dream and the physical characteristics of the members of the cast, it seemed to me that they were making a picture in their minds of how it looked and felt to be in my dream and were probably preparing to play a part in it. Even before I finished my description, they both wanted to be the swooping Brazen Hussy.

If you have been following along with your own dream and there are people you trust who are available to you, you are ready to cast the play. If you aren't sure who you want in a part, ask for volunteers. If there is no one for a particular part, you can play the part yourself. You don't need to be limited to human roles as you cast. In my sample dream, I could have cast someone in the role of tote bag, ganglia, or any other objects or elements that were part of my dream. And one person can play more than one part. You may want to cast someone to be a backup or advocate for yourself if you find yourself in trouble. You can use a backup whenever you want, much the way the Senoi call in allies to help them in their fantasies or dreams.

There are popular roles and unpopular roles. The popular roles are generally those with socially approved, admirable characteristics, and the unpopular ones, those with disdained, unattractive characteristics. Playing an unpopular role is actually more rewarding because it forces us to recognize and use characteristics in ourselves that we don't like and don't want to admit we have. Finding and using those traits helps us to come to terms with ourselves, to be more comfortable in our own skins. Psychodrama, in any event, usually offers actors an opportunity to change roles before the play is over.

Since both of my group members wanted to be the Brazen Hussy, I suggested that they play that part in turn. Unexpected rewards are reaped by both playing a role and then watching somebody else play it. The drama can be replayed and rewoven as many times as the group and the dreamer want.

We used an empty chair to represent Barbara because her character didn't pose a problem for me. We used asides to comment briefly on the action, and whenever anyone wanted to talk at greater length about what was happening or to switch roles, we froze the action and allowed that person to soliloquize.

In the first enactment, Pat plays Goody Two-Shoes, Dorothy plays Brazen Hussy and I play myself. Pat tells me how wicked I am to want the things I want. She assigns me a whole history of inappropriate conduct, which she details. She talks a long time while I cower. I turn to ask her to stop. "What do you want from me?" She goes on and on. [Interestingly enough, I can't remember much of the content.] I cover my ears and put my head in my lap. Pat just moves in closer and talks louder. I can't seem to bring myself to face her, although I think about it. I finally find myself calling, "Swooper (another name for the Brazen Hussy), when are you going to swoop?" I invoke the Swooper to come to my aid as a helper, an auxiliary ego, to do what I can't do and to protect me from Goody Two-Shoes, who is getting too mean.

The role of helper does not need to be part of the dream plot. Or it may be. The protagonist can stop the action and direct someone to provide help from outside the dream plot or call upon one of the already cast characters to advance the plot. I called the Swooper to help me by performing her role in the drama. If she had not come, or if Goody Two-Shoes's attack had been too painful for me to bear, I could have stopped the action, changed the script or switched to the attacking or the swooping role myself. Changing the plot of a dream (and it always is somewhat changed in its reenactment) opens up the possibility of changing your overly compelling life script.

"Please come soooon!" I howl. To my surprise, Pat also wants Dorothy, the Swooper, to swoop. The Swooper seems to delay a long time, although she is poised for action. Finally, when both Pat and I begin to plead, she swoops in, to our relief.

After a while we change roles, and with each change the group becomes more excited and interested. At the end of each enactment, each player talks a little about what it was like to play the assigned part.

When Dorothy plays Goody Two-Shoes she realizes that she wants, even more than Margot, to know what is in the bag. It is her urge to discover that creates mean, anti-urge talk. Her experience rings true for me, too. Goody is just as relieved as Margot when the Swooper swoops, but she gives lip service to a different feeling in order to retain her "virtue."

All three of us well-brought-up, middle-aged women love being the Swooper, a part of ourselves that has fallen into disuse. Possibilities that we have not recognized in ourselves open up for all of us. And we have a lot of fun.

While there are many more insights to be gained from this small segment of a dream drama, this gives you an idea of how psychodrama is done. Using even a small excerpt from a dream as a starting place, you will have no trouble playing the dream, elaborating on it, or changing it once people begin to play. This kind of work never dies of lethargy, but it can be an extremely powerful arouser of painful old emotions; therefore, it must be treated with caution and not be allowed to get out of hand. Never make anyone play an unwanted role, and be sure everyone feels comfortable about backing out at any moment. If your actors are at ease, they will be able to bring creativity and spontaneity to the process of opening up new possibilities to the dreamer and to themselves.

Worksheet
Dream Theater

Title of Dream _____

Written and directed by _____
                          (the Dreamer)

The Skeleton of the Action:
(Summarize the plot and setting of your dream here.)

Cast of Characters:

Character	Name of him, her or it	Played by
Protagonist	_____	_____
	_____	_____
Auxiliary Egos (the Good Guys)	_____	_____
	_____	_____
Antagonist	_____	_____
	_____	_____
Alter Egos (the Bad Guys)	_____	_____
	_____	_____
Supporting Cast	_____	_____
	_____	_____

Postimprovisation feelings about the drama:

Protagonist:

Auxiliary ego:

Antagonist:

Alter ego:

Supporting characters:

Questions for the dreamer to ask him or herself:
How do I feel about the dream now?

What changes took place in the dream as it unfolded?

What is the relationship of the dream characters to each other?

To my life?

And things for the other members of the group to ask themselves:
What are my own answers to the above dreamer's questions?

Further Resources

You may find that you would like someone to guide or accompany you. The following is a short list of networking organizations that you may contact. If you should want to start a dream group of your own with other people who are interested in exploring and sharing their dream experiences, these organizations can give you guidance or resources.

A group that studies dreams:

Association for the Study of Dreams
Master Organization
P.O. Box 1600
Vienna, VA 22183
703-242-8888

An international, multidisciplinary professional organization that has information on anything you could ever want to know or even imagine about dreams. It also prints a bimonthly newsletter and sponsors an annual conference. These conferences present the latest research on dreams and also include workshops, art shows, films, poetry and various other dream-related offerings. A good time is usually had by all, and there is something for everyone.

For Problem Solving with Dreams:

Gayle Delaney, Ph.D., and Loma K. Flowers, M.D.
Professional Dream and Consultation Center
337 Spruce Street
San Francisco, CA 94118

This group runs workshops and a monthly group, does individual consultations and counseling, all of extremely high quality.

For psychoanalytic (Freudian) approaches, contact any psychoanalytic training institute located in the large city nearest you. It will almost certainly have courses open to the general public, probably not specifically directed toward dreams, but expounding an approach that can be used to analyze your dreams.

For Jungian and Senoi dream work:

Jungian-Senoi Institute
P.O. Box 9036
Berkeley, CA 94709

Offers a dream work correspondence course based on the Williams manual (see Bibliography above) plus several in-house courses and therapy.

For Gestalt dream work, contact any Gestalt institute or therapist in your area.

For referrals to those who do physical work with dreams, you may write to:

Gene Gendlin
Department of Behavioral Sciences
Committee of Methodology of Behavioral Research
3848 South University Avenue
Chicago, IL 60637

Sometimes massage therapists or Feldenkrais therapists can steer you to someone who knows bioenergetics (the discipline on which this practice is based).

For Dream Theater:

American Society for Group Psychotherapy and Psychodrama
6728 Old McLean Village Drive
McLean, VA 22101
703-556-9222

Or to find someone licensed in Psychodrama in your area:

American Board of Examiners in Psychodrama, Sociometry
and Group Psychotherapy
P.O. Box 15572
Washington, DC 200003

For couples workshops, workshops on creativity for families and other workshops that use dreams and psychodrama:

Allan Wickersty, Ph.D., T.E.P.
6101 Kilmer Street
Cheverly, MD 20785

Bibliography

If you want to delve more deeply into any of the approaches presented here, this is a short but representative bibliography.

Chapter I: Problem-Solving Dreams

Delaney, Gayle. *Living Your Dreams, Using Your Sleep to Solve Problems and to Make Your Best Dreams Come True.* New York: Harper and Row, 1979. The definitive work on using dreams to solve problems.

Chapter II: The Senoi

Stewart, Kilton. "Dream Theory." From *Fire*, summer, 1967. A clear, though idealized description of how the Senoi live, dream and treat their dreams by the psychoanalytically trained anthropologist who first brought this tribe to the attention of Western scholars.

Chapter III: Freud

Freud, Sigmund. *The Interpretation of Dreams.* New York: Avon, 1965. Freud's earliest (1900) formation of psychoanalysis and an exhaustive study of dreams. It extensively reviews the literature on dreams up to that point. Fascinating reading for anyone interested in dreams or psychoanalysis.

_____ . *An Outline of Psychoanalysis.* Lytton Strachey, ed. New York: W. W. Norton, 1949. One of Freud's last works. The chapter, "Dream Interpretation as an Illustration," illustrates the unfolding of Freud's ideas of the unconscious and the mechanisms of drive theory as they are shown in dreams. This book requires some knowledge of the principles of psychoanalysis. It is rich material.

Fromm, Erich. *Dreams, the Forgotten Language.* New York: Grove Press, 1980. A clear, concise and sensitive review of how dreams have been viewed historically up through psychoanalysis by a well known psychoanalyst and one of the first psychoanalytic interpreters of history (*Escape from Freedom*) including Fromm's own ways of working with dreams.

Chapter IV: Jung

Jung, C. G. *The Portable Jung.* New York: Viking, 1971. A compendium of Jung's works, edited, interpreted and introduced by

Joseph Campbell. Translated by R. F. C. Hull.

Sanford, John A. *Dreams and Healing, A Succinct and Lively Interpretation of Dreams*. New York: Paulist Press, 1978.

Williams, Strephon. *Jungian-Senoi Dreamwork Manual*. Berkeley: Journey Press, 1980. An eclectic approach to dreams that leans toward the Jungian and the Senoi theories, with emphasis on dreams as a means of spiritual development.

Chapter V: Gestalt

Downing, Jack, and Robert Marmorstein, eds. *Dreams and Nightmares*. New York: Harper and Row, 1973. Includes play-by-play verbatim descriptions of a finely tuned therapist helping people work with their dreams.

Perls, Fritz. *The Gestalt Approach and Eye Witness to Therapy*. Palo Alto: Science and Behavior Books, 1973. More examples of working with dreams by a master of dream work.

Chapter VI: Body Methods

Lowen, Alexander. *The Betrayal of the Body*. London: MacMillan, 1969. The original text on bioenergetics, not specifically geared to dreams but applicable to them.

Gendlin, Eugene T. *Let Your Body Interpret Your Dreams*. Wilmette, IL: Chiron, 1986. An original approach to sensory awareness as a way of learning about dreams.

Chapter VII: Dream Theater

Moreno, Jacob. *Psychodrama*. New York: Beacon House, 1964. Not specifically geared to dreams but to any lifescript drama that can be easily applied to dream work.